CULTURE Champions

Teachers Supporting a Healthy School Culture

Edited by
ANTHONY MUHAMMAD

Solution Tree | Press
a division of Solution Tree

555 North Morton Street
Bloomington, IN 47404
800.733.6786 (toll free) / 812.336.7700
FAX: 812.336.7790

email: info@SolutionTree.com
SolutionTree.com

Visit **go.SolutionTree.com/schoolimprovement** to download the free reproducibles in this book.

Printed in the United States of America

Library of Congress Cataloging-in-Publication Data

Names: Muhammad, Anthony, editor.
Title: Culture champions : teachers supporting a healthy classroom culture / Anthony Muhammad, editor.
Description: Bloomington, IN : Solution Tree Press, 2025. | Includes bibliographical references and index.
Identifiers: LCCN 2024034290 (print) | LCCN 2024034291 (ebook) | ISBN 9781962188104 (paperback) | ISBN 9781962188111 (ebook)
Subjects: LCSH: Classroom environment. | Classroom management. | Motivation in education. | Teachers--Professional relationships.
Classification: LCC LB3013 .C834 2025 (print) | LCC LB3013 (ebook) | DDC 371.102/4--dc23/eng/20241015
LC record available at https://lccn.loc.gov/2024034290
LC ebook record available at https://lccn.loc.gov/2024034291

Solution Tree
Jeffrey C. Jones, CEO
Edmund M. Ackerman, President

Solution Tree Press
President and Publisher: Douglas M. Rife
Associate Publishers: Todd Brakke and Kendra Slayton
Editorial Director: Laurel Hecker
Art Director: Rian Anderson
Copy Chief: Jessi Finn
Senior Production Editor: Suzanne Kraszewski
Copy Editor: Jessica Starr
Proofreader: Charlotte Jones
Text and Cover Designer: Laura Cox
Acquisitions Editors: Carol Collins and Hilary Goff
Content Development Specialist: Amy Rubenstein
Associate Editors: Sarah Ludwig and Elijah Oates
Editorial Assistant: Anne Marie Watkins

Acknowledgments

I want to thank all the wonderful contributors to this book for sharing their experiences, insights, and expertise with others in the field. Each author in this anthology is a star. Education is a profession, and the more we share what works with one another, the brighter our future will be.

I want to thank the staff at Solution Tree Press for partnering to make this book a reality. Solution Tree Press has been a pioneer in promoting practitioner-driven literature. For many of the authors in this anthology, it is their first time as a published author, but I am sure it will not be their last. Thanks for providing the resources, care, and guidance to make this book a reality.

Finally, I want to thank the readers. A book is only as important as its impact. I want to thank every educator who takes the time to read the experiences and guidance shared in this book. It is only when educators—teachers in particular—understand how to use the power of positive influence that we will truly ensure every school has a healthy culture.

—Anthony Muhammad

Visit **go.SolutionTree.com/schoolimprovement** to download the free reproducibles in this book.

Table of Contents

About the Editor

Anthony Muhammad, PhD, is an author and international thought leader. He is considered one of the world's leading experts in the areas of school culture and Professional Learning Communities at Work®. He has been honored by the Global Gurus organization as one of the thirty most influential education thought leaders in the world in 2021, 2022, and 2023. Dr. Muhammad served as a middle school teacher and administrator for nearly twenty years, and he received several formal awards in both roles.

As a researcher, Dr. Muhammad has published articles in several publications. He is the author of *The Way Forward: PLC at Work and the Bright Future of Education*, *Transforming School Culture: How to Overcome Staff Division*, and *Overcoming the Achievement Gap Trap: Liberating Mindsets to Effect Change*. He is a coauthor of *Revisiting Professional Learning Communities at Work: Proven Insights for Sustained, Substantive School Improvement (Second Edition)*; *The Will to Lead, the Skill to Teach: Transforming Schools at Every Level*; and *Time for Change: Four Essential Skills for Transformational School and District Leaders*. Dr. Muhammad is also a contributor to *Beyond Conversations About Race: A Guide for Discussions With Students, Teachers, and Communities* and *The Collaborative Administrator: Working Together as a Professional Learning Community*, and he is the editor of *Culture Keepers: Leaders Creating a Healthy School Culture*.

To learn more about Dr. Muhammad's work, visit New Frontier 21 (www.newfrontier21.com), or follow @newfrontier21 on X, formerly known as Twitter.

To book Anthony Muhammad for professional development, contact pd@SolutionTree.com.

Preface

By Anthony Muhammad

It has always been my dream that every school would be a place where all students can thrive. That school would be a place where every educator was flexible, empathetic, student-centered, and highly skilled. Student failure of any sort would bother all educators deeply. I have experienced pieces of this dream in my over-thirty-year career, but rarely have I seen it as the overwhelming institutional norm.

I am a proud student of Rober Eaker and the late Richard DuFour and the Professional Learning Communities (PLC) at Work process of school improvement. This process advocates for teachers to work together on critical areas of practice—including curriculum, assessment, and intervention—all with a focus on improving student learning. I firmly believe that PLC at Work provides the best road map for positive impact on student learning and holistic development. I was fortunate to become an associate in 2003 and a surrogate of the process that Bob and Rick crafted.

As I brought the tenants of the PLC at Work process to schools across the United States, I experienced an alarming level of variance in implementation. Some schools were immediately attracted to the big ideas of the process. They were willing to consider this radically different approach and wrestle with their own dissonance for the benefit of their students. In other places, the opposite reality existed—I encountered educators who were defensive, resistant, and sometimes even hostile. This dichotomy puzzled me.

As a young consultant, I started to doubt whether my passion for the PLC at Work process was misplaced. Perhaps there was a flaw in the system I had not detected, or maybe there was something flawed about some of the environments or cultures where I sought to influence practice. Certainly, if a valid innovation can be effective in one system, that impact could be duplicated in a similar system, right? After deep reflection, I decided to lean on the assumption that good practices have the highest probability of success when they are implemented within the context of a strong and positive organizational culture.

I started to look at school improvement as a two-tiered phenomenon. I theorized that the first tier of improvement is considered technical, encompassing the nonhuman components of the system, like curriculum, strategies, and technology. I referred to the technical level of change in a system as *the skill*. The second level of organizational change, which I would discover later was by far the most challenging, is the cultural level. This would address the complexity of human behavior, including attitudes, dispositions, habits, norms, and behaviors. I refer to this level of change as *the will*. If schools are to truly improve, they would need to evolve at the *will* and *skill* level (Muhammad & Hollie, 2011). There is plenty of scholarship in the education field on the technical level of school improvement; I became obsessed with influencing how to intentionally and methodically improve school culture.

The study of school culture goes back to the 20th century. The oldest scholarly work on the topic can be traced to a book titled *The Sociology of Teaching* by educational sociology researcher Willard Waller (1932). Waller saw schools as a network of social interactions between Innovators and Traditionalists fighting for control of the organization's ideological direction. Education professor Dan C. Lortie added a significant contribution in 1975 with his seminal work titled *School Teacher: A Sociological Study*. Lortie (1975) theorized that educators were socialized into their profession in much different ways than other professionals. He concluded that most educators had been socialized in their field of education since early childhood, where they observed standard professional operating procedures as students. He called this unique experience the apprenticeship of observation. According to Lortie (1975), this experience biased educators to traditions in their field in a unique way compared to other professionals. Educational leadership researchers Terrence E. Deal and Kent D. Peterson (1999) later catalyzed the empirical analysis of school culture in their book *Shaping School Culture: The Heart of Leadership*. These authors defined school culture as a construct that could not only be observed, but also strategically shaped and formed.

As an active school professional since 1990, I have witnessed the struggle to substantively improve school performance. I've seen one technical change after another fail before it was even fully launched. I theorized that the underdevelopment of school culture was the primary culprit for the failure of school improvement. In 2006, I launched a study of thirty-four different schools and an analysis of the health of their cultures; this research later became part of *Transforming School Culture: How to Overcome Staff Division,* which was first published in 2009 (Muhammad, 2009).

In my study of these thirty-four schools and how their educators (teachers, counselors, administrators, and support staff) interacted in the school culture and articulated their beliefs through their behavior, I found a war of belief systems very similar to Waller's observation in 1932. I found four distinct ideological subcultures actively engaged in a battle to make their belief system the norm of the school. Two critical subculture groups (those Waller [1932] labeled *Traditionalists* and *Innovators*) had distinct characteristics and "weapons" (behaviors and tools) that they used to exercise their influence on the school culture. A third group found itself innocently in the center of the battle, and a fourth group, simply trying to survive the school day, was a casualty of the persistent battle. These four groups and their characteristics had a divisive impact on the school culture. I determined that to transform from a toxic to a healthy learning environment, it was essential for leaders to understand and influence change within these groups of educators.

I call the first group the Believers. *Believers* are educators who believe in the core values that make up a healthy school culture. They believe that all their students are capable of learning and that they have a direct impact on student success. They are actively engaged in a constant battle concerning innovation with another group, the Fundamentalists.

The second group I call the Tweeners. *Tweeners* are educators who are new to the school culture. Their experience can be likened to a honeymoon period in which they spend time trying to learn the norms and expectations of the school's culture. They end up in the middle of the war of ideas between the Believers and Fundamentalists.

The third group I identify are the *Survivors.* Unfortunately, the prevalence of this group has increased since originally publishing this research in 2009.

They represent the profile of educators that some would consider burned out—so overwhelmed by the profession's demands that they suffer from depression and merely survive from day to day. Toxic cultures and poor working conditions contribute to the development of this subculture of educators. I consider them victims of circumstance.

The fourth group I call the Fundamentalists. *Fundamentalists* are staff members who are not only opposed to change but also organize to resist and thwart any change that threatens their personal comfort and security. They often wield tremendous political power in toxic cultures and are a major obstacle in implementing meaningful school reform. They actively work against the Believers.

I found that schools in which Believers were active, influential, and engaged in shaping the school's culture daily forged a culture of growth, innovation, and optimism. The power to shape culture is in our hands if we accept the challenge. In fact, if I were to recreate the framework today, I would rename Believers, instead calling them Unapologetic Child Advocates.

This book is dedicated to the advocacy, influence, and efficacy of Believers. It will provide you with insight, strategies, and tools to help you positively influence the culture of your classroom, team, school, and district if you are willing to take on this challenge. I hope that you take the sage advice offered in this collection of solutions and make your environment, and our profession, a healthy place for all kids to thrive.

References and Resources

Deal, T. E., & Peterson, K. D. (1999). *Shaping school culture: The heart of leadership*. San Fransisco: Jossey-Bass.

Lortie, D. C. (1975). *Schoolteacher: A sociological study*. Chicago: University of Chicago Press.

Muhammad, A. (2009). *Transforming school culture: How to overcome staff division.* Bloomington, IN: Solution Tree Press.

Muhammad, A. (2017). *Transforming school culture: How to overcome staff division* (2nd ed.). Bloomington, IN: Solution Tree Press.

Muhammad, A., & Hollie, S. (2011). *The will to lead, the skill to teach: Transforming schools at every level.* Bloomington, IN: Solution Tree Press.

Waller, W. (1932). *The sociology of teaching*. New York: Wiley.

Luis F. Cruz, PhD, is a sought-after presenter, coach, thought leader, and accomplished author in the education field. His over thirty years of practical experience as a teacher and administrator at the elementary, middle, and high school levels, coupled with his ability to effectively communicate research-based approaches focused on ensuring high levels of learning for all students, has earned him acknowledgment and praise from an array of education communities around the United States.

Born to immigrant parents from South America, Dr. Cruz blends his experience as an English learner raised in a low-income community in Los Angeles with his professional insight to advocate for public school educators to acknowledge that there is a disconnect between our inherited, antiquated public school system and today's diverse student population. He, therefore, advocates that public school educators learn and commit to redesigning a school system that ensures high levels of learning for all students in classrooms across the United States.

In addition to being an accomplished and highly desired keynote speaker, Dr. Cruz has established a skilled and effective manner for helping audiences, both small and large, learn about PLC at Work and Response to Intervention at Work™ processes, transformational leadership, school culture, and the role of a guiding coalition in creating environments conducive to the success of students learning English as an additional language. These are a few of the professional development themes for which he is contracted.

Dr. Cruz is the best-selling author of *Time for Change: Four Essential Skills for Transformational School and District Leaders*, which he coauthored with Dr. Anthony Muhammad. He is also a coauthor of the second edition of *Taking Action: A Handbook for RTI at Work* and a contributing author to *It's About Time: Planning Intervention and Extensions in Secondary School.* His next book will focus on enhancing learning outcomes for emergent multilingual students.

To learn more about Luis Cruz's work, follow @lcruzconsulting on X.

To book Luis Cruz for professional development, contact pd@SolutionTree.com.

CHAPTER 1

Responding to Peers Who Have Lost Their Way

By Luis F. Cruz

Principal Hernandez could not understand why his staff members were so resistant to his proposed changes. Even though more than half of his staff had attended conferences regarding how best to enhance learning for the middle school students they served, they were still not on board with the needed changes. In fact, a grievance on behalf of the teachers had been filed that challenged several of Principal Hernandez's directives, including the following.

1. A decision to require agendas for teacher collaboration that administration would review beforehand
2. A new protocol for analyzing common assessments that Principal Hernandez himself created to save teachers' time
3. A change proposed to the master schedule aimed at creating time during the contractual day for intervention

Principal Hernandez had asked teachers at the end of the academic year if they agreed that more needed to be done to help students succeed academically; to his delight, most of the staff agreed. He spent the whole summer making these changes only to have the staff reject his well-intended leadership with a formal grievance. Where did Principal Hernandez go wrong?

Improving schools to generate continuous evidence of student learning is a long and arduous process. However, the countless hours, philosophical feuds, and emotionally fueled interactions with internal and external stakeholders are worth every bit of struggle when a growing number of students leave schools with the knowledge and skills required for success. Since 1989, I have served students in communities of poverty as an instructional aide, teacher, and administrator at the elementary, middle, and high school levels and today as a consultant and author. These rich experiences have generated some undeniable truths about school improvement dynamics not found in teaching or administrative credential courses.

- The hardest part of improvement is not in interactions with students, but in interactions with other adults.
- Effective leadership in schools can no longer be synonymous with only school principals.
- Teachers have more influence on staff to embrace change than administrators do.

This chapter attempts to unveil an untapped source and impetus for change: teacher leadership. Thus, there is a need to prepare teachers to lead change initiatives in schools by providing them with a vital prerequisite for success: the ability to effectively communicate *why* it is critical to embrace uncomfortable change initiatives that accelerate student learning (Muhammad & Cruz, 2019). In short, establishing a healthy school culture focused on high levels of learning for all students is not sustainable without teacher leadership.

First, this chapter sets the foundation for communicating the why by introducing a great challenge educators face and how to overcome it using research-based practices. Then, this chapter defines the importance of teacher leadership in the change process, particularly to address teachers' cognitive rationale for resisting change. A link between leadership and the influence it has on adult behavior must be clearly established considering that a school's culture is a result of the collective behavior that staff embrace or reject. Without understanding this symbiotic relationship between leadership and required adult behaviors, establishing a healthy school culture is left to chance instead of determined by intentional design. Finally, this chapter concludes with four approaches teacher leaders, as transformational leaders, can use to effect change.

The Challenge Facing Education

It has taken over three decades of work as a public school educator for me to realize the obvious: the greatest challenge the public school system faces is keeping pace with ever-evolving societal changes. For example, when shifts in economic structures, technological advances, and political rhetoric emerge in society, such changes will affect the way schools conduct the business of teaching and learning. As a result, educators must continuously manage the skills and knowledge necessary for students to be successful. Educational policy and leadership professor David Conley (2017) determines that college-bound students require specific skill sets to be successful. He also distinguishes between students earning admission to college, which typically requires a certain grade point average, a specific score on the SAT or ACT entrance exams, and the skills to succeed once enrolled. For example, some of the prerequisite skills he identifies are drawing inferences and conclusions from texts, supporting arguments with evidence, using persuasive writing, and solving complex problems with no obvious solutions (Conley, 2017). Similarly, the World Economic Forum (2020), a nongovernmental organization that initiates public-private sector collaboration and studies world economic trends, identifies complex problem solving, creativity, originality, analysis, resilience, stress tolerance, and flexibility as instrumental for individuals seeking alternative paths to success, such as trades. The revelation of these essential skills will challenge educators to confront the likelihood that our antiquated public school system is not equipped to ensure students leave schools with the necessary skills to be successful. As a result, changing the current public school system (policies, practices, and procedures) to ensure the students we serve acquire the knowledge and skills necessary to access paths to success must become a focal point for school leaders. Thus, to support students in acquiring the necessary knowledge and skills for success, professional school educators must commit to using research-based practices in the classroom and throughout the school.

When I come across noneducators who articulate a somewhat thwarted belief that teaching is easy and something they can surely do, I am quick to define professional school educators. As professional school educators, we are expected to align our skill sets with research-based best practices that produce evidence of learning for the students we serve (Marzano, 2017). The goal, then, is identifying and implementing these research-based practices that have the power to advance student learning. While this process may sound somewhat simplistic, changing adult behavior—especially the behavior of those who work in schools—will be challenging (Muhammad, 2018). Leadership author and speaker John Maxwell (2020) captures this thinking best when he states that for organizations in search of excellence, like schools, members will have to realize that, while change is inevitable, growth is optional. Teachers commit to helping all students succeed when they commit to changing their instructional methods to incorporate research-based practices.

The Importance of Research-Based Practices

In *Visible Learning: The Sequel—A Synthesis of Over 2,100 Meta-Analyses Relating to Achievement*, education researcher John Hattie (2023) synthesizes research-based best practices for student learning. Based on 2,100 meta-analyses of over 130,000 studies involving 400 million students, Hattie (2023) identifies the effect school-based actions and behaviors have on student learning. Using a barometer of influence, Hattie (2023) showcases the degree of influence of specific effects—reverse, developmental, teacher, or zone of desired effects. While Hattie (2023) identifies over 350 of these influences on student learning, the behaviors and effect sizes in the zone of desired effects are of particular interest. Hattie (2023) concludes that school actions within the zone of desired effects, particularly those with a 1.0 standard deviation, have the potential to produce two to three years of learning for students within one school year. The strongest influence on student learning, with a standard deviation of 1.34, is collective teacher efficacy, a process whereby teachers collectively believe their students can demonstrate learning and work collaboratively to implement best practices. Since Hattie started his research on achievement in 2008, collective teacher efficacy has consistently ranked as the strongest influence on student learning (Hattie, 2009, 2023). Collective teacher efficacy is best captured within the context of the Professional Learning Community (PLC) at Work® process.

Since 1998, the PLC at Work process has offered schools research-based strategies for sustained, substantive school improvement (DuFour & Eaker, 1998). According to educational researcher Richard DuFour and colleagues (2024), it is:

> An ongoing process in which educators work collaboratively in recurring cycles of collective inquiry and action research to achieve better results for the students they serve. PLCs operate under the assumption that the key to improved learning for students is continuous job embedded learning for educators. (p. 14)

Further, DuFour and colleagues (2024) identify non-negotiable, "tight" actions that are required for the PLC process to effectively generate optimal student learning. Briefly, these are the actions teacher teams must initiate.

1. Take collective responsibility for student learning.
2. Establish a guaranteed and viable curriculum by collaboratively identifying essential standards.
3. Create common formative assessments to assess learning as a result of classroom instruction.
4. Analyze common formative assessments to identify students in need of additional support and identify effective instructional practices among team members.
5. Use the data from common formative assessments to create a systematic response in the form of intervention when students do not learn the agreed-on essential standards.

It is important to note that each of these tight actions is dependent on the will and work of teachers. This is an important observation that will fuel the necessity to discuss teacher leadership later in this chapter.

In *The Way Forward: PLC at Work and the Bright Future of Education*, education consultant and author Anthony Muhammad (2024) makes a compelling case as to why the PLC at Work process must act as a catalyst to achieve continuous evidence of student learning, especially in the aftermath of the global COVID-19 pandemic. Muhammad (2024) states the following:

> We can do better, and the pathways to a more effective school system existed long before the global pandemic, but the lack of collective efficacy within the field of education allowed us to intellectually admire those better practices without making a full collective commitment to embrace and implement them. I argue that the best of those better pathways is the PLC at Work process. If we dare take another look at this process, which has been around since 1998, we could make the post-COVID era much more promising than the reality before March 2020. (p. 20)

Thus far, I have made the case that educators face the critical challenge of being unable to provide students with the knowledge and skills they require to be successful in today's fast-paced world. Fortunately, as professional educators, our field has identified a preponderance of research-based best practices that positively influence student learning. When implemented effectively, collective teacher efficacy, such as through the PLC at Work process, has a positive impact on student achievement (Hattie, 2023). However, Muhammad's (2018) extensive work on transforming school culture demonstrates that necessary change in schools generates resistance. While transformational leadership is an effective approach for organizational change, teachers must embrace non-negotiables and professionally challenge peers who resist change before moving forward (Muhammad & Cruz, 2019). As mentioned earlier in this chapter, creating a healthy school culture happens when educators commit to uncomfortable changes in their collective behavior for the purpose of accelerating student learning. Initiating this process requires momentum. This is where teacher leadership comes in.

The Critical Role of Teacher Leadership

Developmental psychologist Howard Gardner (2004, 2024) provides an array of reasons and approaches explaining why and how human thinking can change. Gardner (2004, 2024) introduces seven strategies for changing someone's mind. The two that are particularly relevant to teacher leadership are: (1) reasoning and rational thinking (the irrefutable evidence that there is a better way of achieving a desired outcome) and (2) resonance (or positive peer pressure). Gardner's (2004, 2024) strategies have been instrumental in persuading staff to commit to improvement initiatives, like the PLC process (DuFour & DuFour, 2012; DuFour, DuFour, Eaker, Mattos, & Muhammad, 2021; DuFour et al., 2024). While the research on collective teacher efficacy and the power of PLCs serves as irrefutable evidence that stronger student achievement outcomes are plausible when schools invest in these practices with depth and duration, positive peer pressure can play an important role in effectively implementing change. Consequently, if implementing the PLC process requires teachers to make an array of changes to how they work together, analyze data, and collectively respond when students do not learn, then positive peer pressure in the form of teacher leadership will be necessary for success.

Authors Kenneth Leithwood, Alma Harris, and David Hopkins (2020) remind us that while school leadership influences a staff's capacity to change, it is teachers who are significant change agents in and beyond the classroom (Darling-Hammond, Hyler & Gardner, 2017). In addition, while the benefits of teacher leadership have been linked to increases in student achievement, they have also been linked to job satisfaction and, most notably, to teacher commitment to school change (Nguyen, Harris, & Ng, 2020; Schott, van Roekel, & Tummers, 2020). If effectively implementing the PLC process depends on teachers changing the way they help students learn, then teachers must play an active role in leading the change process among their peers. If teachers are not included in the leadership process, then the most likely outcome will be a short-lived fad and not the necessary movement required to continuously elevate student learning (Hall, 2022). In short, effective leadership in schools can no longer be synonymous with only administration. Since school environments are not conducive to immediately embrace change (Muhammad & Cruz, 2019), the challenge is ensuring that teachers possess the skill set required to lead and influence fellow colleagues to engage in the practices that are critical to student achievement. In other words, if establishing a healthy school culture is paramount to integrating research-based practices aligned with student learning, then teacher leadership will act as a vital resource leading to the creation of such a culture. Furthermore, teacher leaders will need to be transformational leaders to create a culture where teachers leverage positive peer pressure to commit to best practices.

Teacher Leaders as Transformational Leaders

In its simplest form, leadership is the ability to influence others to follow. Individuals who influence others to follow them and change their behaviors possess leadership characteristics. In schools, leadership represents "the ability to use influence to improve organizational productivity" (Muhammad & Cruz, 2019, p. 2). While an array of leadership styles have been tested over the years, transformational leadership is necessary in schools seeking to embrace change for improved productivity, defined as increases in student achievement. First introduced in 1978, transformational leadership requires leaders to acknowledge the needs of people inside their organizations to propel behavioral changes. A Langston University (2016) paper best captures this idea:

> Transformational leadership is defined as a leadership approach that causes change in individuals and social systems. In its ideal form, it creates valuable and positive change in the followers with the end goal of developing followers into leaders. Enacted in its authentic form, transformational leaders enhance the motivation, morale, and performance of followers through a variety of mechanisms. (p. 1)

In *Time for Change: Four Essential Skills for Transformational School and District Leaders*, education consultants Anthony Muhammad and Luis F. Cruz (2019) attempt to expand the tenets of transformational leadership by identifying four of those mechanisms: (1) the *why*, (2) the *who*, (3) the *how*, and (4) the *do* of the work. Specifically, there are four essential skills for responding to both rational and irrational forms of resistance to change. To best facilitate change, transformational leaders must balance support and accountability, which the next section discusses.

Support Precedes Accountability

Muhammad and Cruz (2019) articulate that successful transformational leaders balance support and accountability when advocating for change. Specifically, transformational leaders precede accountability with support by investing in three rational needs staff members require to embrace change initiatives. First, when staff members have a *cognitive need* to understand the *why* behind a change initiative, transformational leaders use data to persuade. In short, data help staff members understand why a change in their behavior is required prior to committing. Second, when staff members have unmet *emotional needs* stemming from a lack of trust, transformational leaders couple empathy with credibility to produce a sense of trustworthiness. Third, staff members may lack the knowledge or skills to commit to the proposed changes and, therefore, have an unfulfilled *functional need*. Thus, transformational leaders provide staff members with training to help teachers implement the changes.

Muhammad and Cruz (2019) describe a staff's support for change initiatives as investments, and accountability is a return on that investment. If transformational leaders continuously invest in supporting staff's cognitive, emotional, and functional needs, any remaining resistance is irrational. Any remaining resistance is no longer a result of unfulfilled needs. Rather, it stems from a desire to resist change for the sake of refusing change (Cruz, 2020). As a result, transformational leaders seek a return on all prior investments by tactfully and professionally articulating to irrational resisters the need to comply regardless of their unwillingness to do so. Figure 1.1 illustrates how investing in staff's cognitive, emotional, and functional needs through the four mechanisms of change allows transformational leaders to hold their staff accountable to necessary systemic changes.

As a consultant who trains administrators and teacher leaders across the United States, I find it rewarding to witness transformational leaders display confidence and empowerment when they learn how to promote necessary changes tactfully and effectively in their schools and districts. I am also often reminded that administrators receive very little training for the skills required to

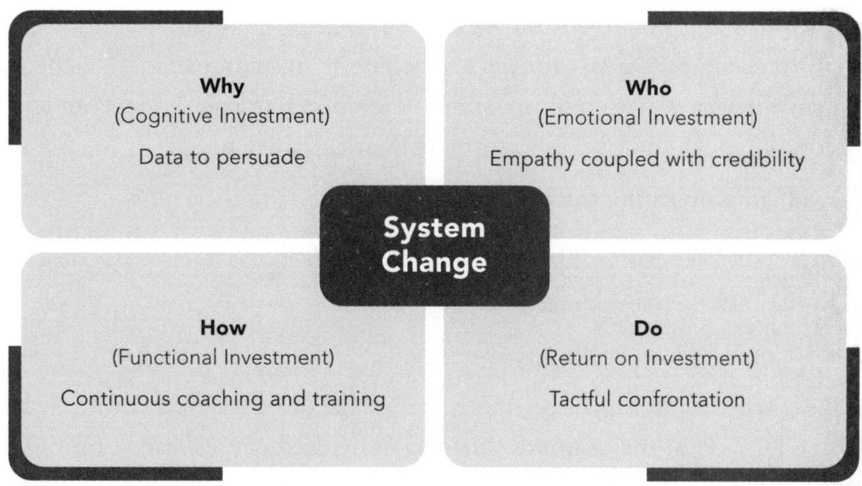

Figure 1.1: Responding to rational resistance.

effectively lead a staff through change initiatives. Reflecting on my own experience and affirmations from current and former administrators, training courses do a more effective job of teaching administrators how to *manage* a school as opposed to *lead* a school as a transformational leader. Thus, for teacher leaders to effectively lead the implementation of research-based practices, such as the PLC process, among their peers, they certainly need to develop the skill sets aligned with transformational leadership.

The most important rational need for teacher leaders to address with their peers is their cognitive need, as communicating the rationale creates an environment conducive to change. By helping their peers fully understand the why behind a change initiative, they are more likely to intrinsically invest in it.

The Importance of Addressing Cognitive Need

Psychologist Frederick Herzberg (1966) reminds leaders that human beings are complex and in need of "stimulation on several different levels in order to unleash their followers' intrinsic commitment" (as cited in Muhammad & Cruz, 2019, p. 24). Thus, one of the most important skill sets transformational leaders use to create an intrinsic commitment to change is communicating the reason *why* a change in practice is needed. As discussed earlier in this chapter, "Transformational leaders must understand how to properly utilize data so that they can inspire intrinsic commitment to a cause bigger than oneself, identify a starting point for improvement, and stimulate personal ownership and internal agency" (Muhammad & Cruz, 2019, p. 27). While Herzberg (1966) refers to this as a *growth-enhancing environment*, psychologist Carol Dweck's (2016) research on *growth mindset* also supports this approach to change. To best encourage a growth mindset among their peers, teacher leaders can leverage four different approaches to support their cognitive needs.

1. Communicating the *institutional why*
2. Communicating the *professional why*
3. Communicating the *societal why*
4. Communicating the *personal why*

While teacher leaders must be trained to use data to effectively communicate change initiatives, these four approaches provide them, as transformational leaders, with an array of skills to influence peers. Table 1.1 captures the unique features of each approach. In the following sections, I describe each approach, identify data teacher leaders can use, and share examples of how these approaches might look in action.

Communicating the Institutional Why

Institutions, like schools, often will develop and declare a purpose—a reason *why* the organization was created and exists. In schools, the purpose for assembling and working together should generate profound behavioral synergy toward achieving a desired outcome: student learning. Schools often reveal their purpose as a mission statement, and this concise written declaration carries the potential to simultaneously clarify priorities and sharpen a staff's focus (DuFour et al., 2024). Therefore, administrators working within the context of a PLC will often purposefully and redundantly communicate the school's mission to students, parents, community members, and especially staff. Consider the following mission statements that schools embrace as a declaration of their purpose.

- **Arvin Union School District (www.arvinschools.com):** "Every child learning, every day, no matter what it takes!"
- **Ball Charter Schools (ballcharterschools.org):** "Provide a personalized education to all students emphasizing comprehensive academic excellence in a safe, nurturing environment through partnering parents, students, and staff."
- **Walnut Valley Unified School District (www.wvusd.org):** "All Walnut Valley students will experience an exceptional education in a supportive, safe, and healthy environment, giving them the skills, ethics, and courage to achieve their dreams in the world of today and tomorrow."

Table 1.1: The Four Whys

The Institutional Why	The Professional Why	The Societal Why	The Personal Why
The institutional why reminds us that no one is an independent contractor. We must all work collaboratively to achieve our school's mission. Questions for teacher leaders to consider when communicating the institutional why include: • Which student achievement data indicate that not all students are learning at high levels? • How committed, both individually and collectively, are we to ensuring all students learn at high levels? • How might we respond based on our data and current level of commitment to achieving our mission?	The professional why reminds us that we, as professional educators, have a responsibility to implement research-based best practices. Questions for teacher leaders to consider when communicating the professional why include: • What research will we use to inform ourselves and best increase student learning? • How will we hold ourselves accountable to use research-based best practices? • How might we link current research to our responsibility as educators to implement best practices?	The societal why reminds us that failure to ensure all students learn at high levels has dire life consequences. Questions for teacher leaders to consider when communicating the societal why include: • What student achievement data indicate that some of our students may be facing life-threatening consequences? • What skills and tools do we have to ensure none of our students become victims of negative statistics? • How might our collective sense of urgency contribute to our implementation of best practices?	The personal why reminds us of our moral imperative and the reasons we became educators. Questions for teacher leaders to consider when communicating the personal why include: • What strategies or tools might we use to share stories, pictures, or artifacts of our journeys to becoming educators? • How might we create a collective space for each of us to share our efforts and successes with the students we serve? • How might we build on our collective moral imperative to strengthen our resolve for implementing best practices?

Source: Adapted from Mattos et al., 2025.

While some mission statements are lengthier than others, the unique characteristics of each focus on *all students* demonstrating evidence of learning. Hence, teacher leaders can articulate the institutional why by reminding their resistant peers that student achievement data do not currently align with the school's mission. Teacher leaders articulating this institutional why is especially important when administrators have done their due diligence and consistently communicated the mission to staff. Teacher leaders communicating the institutional why may sound like the following.

- "Considering that our mission is to ensure learning for all the students we serve, it's concerning that for the last three years we have had a steady decline in the number of students who have not mastered algebra 1 essential standards. It's time we work together as a team, study the problem, and generate more effective solutions."
- "We have made a staff commitment to strive for academic excellence; currently, over half of our fifth-grade student population is transferring to middle school not able to read at grade level. It would behoove us as a team to unveil the cause of this unacceptable outcome and make changes accordingly."
- "Several years ago, our staff created a mission statement focused on every student learning every day, no matter what it takes; therefore, the fact that our students who are learning English as an additional language are graduating at a rate below the general student population is unacceptable. It is time we all participate in being true to our mission."

I use the term *organizational hypocrisy* to describe the phenomena that takes place when organizations declare a purpose but fail to address data indicative of the opposite. When teacher leaders use the school mission statement coupled with data indicative of low evidence of student learning, they articulate a desire to not engage in organizational hypocrisy. After articulating the institutional why, teacher leaders might need to help remind staff that those of us who work in schools are professional educators, not amateurs. This comes in the form of the *professional why*.

Communicating the Professional Why

Earlier in this chapter, I stated that, as professional public school educators, we have a responsibility to adhere to the field's research-based best practices that continuously advance student learning. I also introduced five tight, nonnegotiable actions of the PLC at Work process. When teachers resist adhering to these and other research-based practices, teacher leaders can be a strong asset in reminding their peers of the research supporting specific instructional strategies. The following examples of teacher leaders communicating the professional why to a resistant peer can help teams justify the tight actions of the PLC at Work process (DuFour et al., 2021).

- **Peer resistance:** "Why must we collaborate and take collective responsibility for student learning? I have been teaching for years, and that was never an expectation before."
- **Professional why response:** "At first, I wondered the same thing, but the more I read the research, it became clear there is compelling evidence that a culture of success in schools is more viable when teachers work together. In short, effective teaching today is a team sport. Let's see if working together yields better results."
- **Peer resistance:** "Why do we need to identify essential standards via a guaranteed and viable curriculum? Shouldn't the district do this for teachers?"
- **Professional why response:** "You know, I wondered the same thing, but remember when we were introduced to the effective schools research? Well, effective schools accept responsibility for generating the essential standards they eventually focus on. Why don't we start with one essential standard and build on collectively identifying others over time?"
- **Peer resistance:** "Why do we need to create common assessments? I think it would be better for each teacher to use their own assessments. Don't you?"
- **Professional why response:** "I don't think we have to stop using our own assessments, but by including common assessments in our collective effort to help students learn, we will be able to measure the instructional impact of each teacher's approach. Then, we'll use what is working in our intervention efforts and improve our instruction. How about we start with one common assessment and take it from there?"

Notice that in each of these responses, the teacher leader sandwiched the research in between an opening that acknowledges the rationale for questioning a particular expectation and a suggestion of what to attempt to comply with the research. Once hearing the professional why, resistant peers can only justify continued resistance by offering alternative research. Their inability to produce research supporting a different approach should lead to, at the very least, an attempt to comply.

Thus far, teacher leaders can use both the institutional why and professional why to address peers' resistance to change. However, to create a sense of urgency to meet students' learning needs requires them to communicate the societal why to peers.

Communicating the Societal Why

The data supporting the societal why extends beyond the confines of a school; instead, it includes the impact on society. Transformational leaders, including teacher leaders, must create a sense of urgency by reminding staff what is at stake if students do not learn at high levels. Although these outcomes that negatively affect students—and society at large—are not secret, it's helpful for staff to see how this connects to them not engaging in best practices. The video *Timebomb: The Cost of Dropping Out*, by my colleague and friend Mike Mattos (2017), best demonstrates the cause-and-effect relationship between failing to continuously increase learning for students and those students incurring a lifetime of personal hardships. Some of the data the video shares include the following.

- A student drops out of school every twenty-six seconds (DoSomething.org, 2018a).
- On average, a high school dropout earns $20,241 annually. That is $10,000 less than high school graduates, and over $36,000 less than a college graduate (Lynch, 2013).
- Students who drop out are three times more likely to be unemployed and twice as likely to be working poor (Breslow, 2012).
- Ninety percent of high school dropouts are on welfare (DoSomething.org, 2018a).
- Seventy-five percent of Americans who receive food stamps are functionally illiterate (DoSomething.org, 2018b).
- Young women who drop out are nine times more likely to become single mothers (Lynch, 2013).
- The United States leads the world in incarceration rates, surpassing China and Russia (Collier, 2014).
- Over 80 percent of the incarcerated population are high school dropouts (Lynch, 2013).
- High school dropouts are sixty-three times more likely to be incarcerated than college graduates (Breslow, 2012).
- Three out of five people in American prisons can't read, and 70 percent of those people will return to prison (National Literacy Institute, n.d.).
- Eighty-five percent of all youth in the juvenile court system are functionally illiterate (Begin to Read, n.d.).

- Female high school dropouts will live an average of ten and a half fewer years than those who graduate from high school (Tavernise, 2012).
- Male high school dropouts will live an average of thirteen fewer years (Tavernise, 2016).

Since the video was published in 2017, the statistics have become even more dire, creating an even higher sense of urgency. For example, in 2021, two million students dropped out—over eight hundred thousand more than the video notes (National Center of Education Statistics, n.d.). Further, a 2024 meta-analysis of six hundred studies on adult mortality from fifty-nine countries demonstrates the link between education and life expectancy (Balaj et al., 2024). The research shows that graduating from high school and earning a four-year degree reduces the morality rate by 34 percent (Balaj et al., 2024). This further showcases a link between our failure to generate learning for students and the dire consequences they can face as a result. The following are other notable findings and observations from the study (Balaj et al., 2024).

- Every additional year of schooling reduces mortality by 3 percent.
- Completing more years of schooling reduces the risk of death by any cause.
- Young adults experience the strongest connection between education level and overall health.
- The link between dropping out and mortality is similar to the mortality rate of a decade of drinking five alcoholic drinks or smoking half a pack of cigarettes daily.
- The health benefits from graduating from high school and earning a four-year college degree are similar to the health benefits from eating a balanced diet and exercising regularly.

By using data that demonstrate the consequences students could face if staff do not engage in best practices for student learning, teacher leaders may communicate the societal whys in the following ways.

- "If we work together to engage in practices proven to work when done effectively, we will keep our students from becoming a detrimental statistic. I think it is worth our time to give this a shot, don't you?"
- "I view investment in these practices as an opportunity to help some of our kids break free from the stranglehold of poverty. Aren't our students worth giving this a try?"

- "If we can keep even one of our students from becoming a negative statistic, isn't it worth our time to try implementing these research-based practices?"

Through real, and albeit unfortunate, data demonstrating the devastating link between our inability to produce learning for students and the dire consequences they face as a result, teacher leaders may be able to sway peers who are reluctant to engage in uncomfortable, yet necessary, practices. Tapping into the moral imperative all educators possess will be a feature of the last why: the personal why.

Communicating the Personal Why

Educational consultant and author Michael Fullan describes the moral imperative that drives individuals to want to serve students in schools (Fullan, 2003; Kirtman & Fullan, 2016). Succinctly put, individuals who choose to work in schools, despite infinite challenges, stressful conditions, political pressures, and low salaries, do so because of a natural high from contributing to student success. Unfortunately, over time, many hardworking and well-intentioned educators lose their moral imperative due to challenging conditions that hinder their ability to achieve the desired outcome of student learning they once passionately sought, such as the ever-evolving societal changes noted earlier in this chapter. It is within this space that teacher leaders can use the personal why to regenerate the moral imperative that once thrived and initiate a willingness to engage in efforts focused on student learning. The personal why is qualitative in nature and revolves around memories and stories of a time when a teacher's moral imperative was strong. Teacher leaders can communicate the personal why to invoke those memories in various ways. Teacher leaders are especially pivotal in initiating and leading change through the personal why due to their own personal stories. Doing so helps regenerate the moral imperative that leads teachers to choose the teaching profession. Consider the following scenarios teacher leaders can use to communicate the personal why to their peers.

- Taking time to have fellow teachers share a positive student outcome because of a specific action they took
- Having teachers share the experience that led them to choose the teaching profession
- Having current and former students share how teachers made a positive difference in their lives
- Asking peers to share about a teacher who made a positive impact on their own lives when they were a student

- Having parents of current and former students share how teachers made a positive difference in their children's lives
- Asking administrators to share ways teachers positively contributed to the student and community

Teacher leaders can leverage these personal memories and real-life accounts to engage their peers in new ways and thus foster success for students. By intentionally creating scenarios where teachers recall and are reminded of the positive difference they make in students' lives, teacher leaders generate a stronger commitment to change.

Conclusion

Hardworking and well-intentioned teachers may resist change due to an unfulfilled cognitive need. Teacher leaders can use the four unique approaches outlined in this chapter with their peers to professionally confront the initial resistance to necessary change initiatives. By periodically leveraging the institutional, professional, societal, and personal why, teacher leaders will fulfill their peers' cognitive needs, prompting them to work with administrators to address emotional and functional needs. These four approaches help teams embrace intrinsic commitments to ensure optimal student learning.

Based on previous unsuccessful attempts to initiate change at Martin Luther King Jr. Middle School, Principal Hernandez decided to change his approach. In the past, teachers on the school leadership team conveyed information between administration and the staff. That year, Principal Hernandez decided that teachers on the leadership team would be leaders alongside him. Two weeks prior to the beginning of the school year, teachers on the leadership team met with Principal Hernandez to discuss changes he had in mind for their school. Principal Hernandez created a safe space for teacher leaders to share their opinions and articulate disagreements, creating mutual insight and, as a result, establishing how best to move forward. Teacher leaders agreed that Principal Hernandez would not be the only person addressing the staff when everyone returned to campus for the beginning of the school year. While he would certainly open their first staff meeting of the year with a welcome statement and a reminder of the school's mission, teacher leaders would then share positive learning data as a means of celebrating followed by data that indicated a need for improvement. Together, administration and teacher leaders would then present research and case studies highlighting how schools with similar characteristics and demographics had achieved stronger evidence of learning. Teacher leaders had suggested to Principal Hernandez that, once proposed change initiatives were introduced, the best next step would be to have each teacher leader meet with staff members in small groups and discuss what adjustments to shared changes might need to be made, as well as what specific support the staff would need to embrace proposed changes. Principal Hernandez agreed to this important suggestion.

Over time, most of the staff understood that it was necessary to create agendas for collaborative meetings as an assurance all teams were on the right path toward schoolwide implementation of effective collaboration. The staff felt a sense of empowerment because their suggested adjustments to the original proposed agenda template were accepted and implemented. The same outcomes were experienced with the other proposed changes, and the staff even generated a stronger intervention schedule for consideration. As these changes unfolded throughout the year, both Principal Hernandez and teacher leaders invested in listening to their staff for concerns and suggestions before proceeding. They allotted time throughout the year, especially during the more challenging months, for teachers to share experiences of students benefiting personally and academically from their individual and collective efforts. Principal Hernandez was delighted with their success and was reminded that people are less likely to tear down a bridge they helped build.

References and Resources

Balaj, M., Henson, C. A., Aronsson, A., Aravkin, A., Beck, K., Degail, C., et al. (2024). Effects of education on adult mortality: A global systemic review and meta-analysis. *The Lancet: Public Health, 9*(3), 155–165.

Begin to Read. (n.d.). *Literacy statistics.* Accessed at www.begintoread.com/research/literacystatistics.html on February 29, 2024.

Breslow, J. M. (2012). *By the numbers: Dropping out of high school.* Accessed at www.pbs.org/wgbh/frontline/article/by-the-numbers-dropping-out-of-high-school on February 29, 2024.

Collier, L. (2014, October). *Incarceration nation.* Accessed at www.apa.org/monitor/2014/10/incarceration on February 29, 2024.

Conley, D. T. (2017). The new complexity of readiness for college and careers. In K. L. McClarty, K. D. Mattern, & M. N. Gaertner (Eds.), *Preparing students for college and careers: Theory, measurement, and educational practice* (pp. 11–22). New York: Routledge.

Cruz, L. F. (2020, Winter). The unfamiliar truth about resistance to change in schools. *AllThingsPLC Magazine*, 30–32.

Darling-Hammond, L., Hyler, M. E., & Gardner, M. (2017). *Effective teacher professional development.* Palo Alto, CA: Learning Policy Institute.

DoSomething.org. (2018a, November 16). *11 facts about dropping out.* Accessed at www.dosomething.org/us/facts/11-facts-about-dropping-out on February 29, 2024.

DoSomething.org. (2018b, November 16). *11 facts about literacy in America.* Accessed at www.dosomething.org/us/facts/11-facts-about-literacy-america on February 29, 2024.

DuFour, R., & DuFour, R. (2012). *Essentials for principals: School leader's guide to Professional Learning Communities at Work.* Bloomington, IN: Solution Tree Press.

DuFour, R., DuFour, R., Eaker, R., Many, T. W., & Mattos, M. (2016). *Learning by doing: A handbook for Professional Learning Communities at Work* (3rd ed.). Bloomington, IN: Solution Tree Press.

DuFour, R., DuFour, R., Eaker, R., Many, T. W., Mattos, M., & Muhammad, A. (2024). *Learning by doing: A handbook for Professional Learning Communities at Work* (4th ed.). Bloomington, IN: Solution Tree Press.

DuFour, R., DuFour, R., Eaker, R., Mattos, M., & Muhammad, A. (2021). *Revisiting Professional Learning Communities at Work: Proven insights for sustained, substantive school improvement* (2nd ed.). Bloomington, IN: Solution Tree Press.

DuFour, R., & Eaker, R. (1998). *Professional Learning Communities at Work: Best practices for enhancing student achievement.* Bloomington, IN: Solution Tree Press.

Dweck, C. S. (2016). *Mindset: The new psychology of success* (Updated ed.). New York: Ballantine Books.

Fullan, M. (2003). *The moral imperative of school leadership.* Thousand Oaks, CA: Corwin Press.

Gardner, H. (2004). *Changing minds: The art and science of changing our own and other people's minds.* Boston: Harvard Business School Press.

Gardner, H. (2024). *The essential Howard Gardner on education.* New York: Teachers College Press.

Hall, B. (2022). *Powerful guiding coalitions: How to build and sustain the leadership team in your PLC at Work.* Bloomington, IN: Solution Tree Press.

Hattie, J. (2009). *Visible learning: A synthesis of over 800 meta-analyses related to achievement.* New York: Routledge.

Hattie, J. (2023). *Visible learning: The sequel—A synthesis of over 2,100 meta-analyses relating to achievement.* New York: Routledge.

Herzberg, F. (1966). *Work and the nature of man.* Cleveland, OH: World.

Kirtman, L., & Fullan, M. (2016). *Leadership: Key competencies for whole-system change.* Bloomington, IN: Solution Tree Press.

Langston University. (2016). *Transformational leadership*. Accessed at https://anyflip.com/xpnf/wpik on February 29, 2024.

Leithwood, K., Harris, A., & Hopkins, D. (2020). Seven strong claims about successful school leadership revisited. *School Leadership and Management, 40*(1), 5–22.

Lezotte, L. W., & McKee, K. M. (2002). *Assembly required: A continuous school-improvement system*. Okemos, MI: Effective Schools Products.

Lynch, M. (2013, November 6). *High school dropout rate: Causes and costs*. Accessed at www.edweek.org/education/opinion-high-school-dropout-rate-causes-and-costs/2013/11 on February 29, 2024.

Mattos, M (Writer). (2017). *Timebomb: The cost of dropping out* [Film]. Solution Tree Press.

Mattos, M., Buffum, A., Malone, J., Cruz, L. F., Dimich, N., & Schuhl, S. (2025). *Taking action: A handbook for RTI at Work* (2nd ed.). Bloomington, IN: Solution Tree Press.

Marzano, R. J. (2017). *The new art and science of teaching*. Bloomington, IN: Solution Tree Press.

Maxwell, J. C. (2020). *Wisdom on leadership: 102 quotes to unlock your potential to lead.* Nashville, TN: FaithWords.

Muhammad, A. (2018). *Transforming school culture: How to overcome staff division* (2nd ed.). Bloomington, IN: Solution Tree Press.

Muhammad, A. (2024). *The way forward: PLC at Work and the bright future of education.* Bloomington, IN: Solution Tree Press.

Muhammad, A., & Cruz, L. F. (2019). *Time for change: Four essential skills for transformational school and district leaders*. Bloomington, IN: Solution Tree Press.

National Center of Education Statistics. (n.d.). *Fast facts: Dropout rates*. Accessed at https://nces.ed.gov/fastfacts/display.asp?id=16 on February 29, 2024.

National Literacy Institute. (n.d.). *Literacy statistics 2024–2025*. Accessed at www.thenationalliteracyinstitute.com/literacy-statistics on February 29, 2024.

Nguyen, D., Harris, A., & Ng, D. (2020). A review of the empirical research on teacher leadership (2003–2017): Evidence, patterns, and implications. *Journal of Educational Administration, 58*(1), 60–80.

Schott, C., van Roekel, H., & Tummers, L. G. (2020). Teacher leadership: A systematic review, methodological quality assessment and conceptual framework. *Educational Research Review, 31*, Article 100352.

Tavernise, S. (2012, February 9). *Education gap grows between rich and poor, studies say.* Accessed at www.nytimes.com/2012/02/10/education/education-gap-grows-between-rich-and-poor-studies-show.html?pagewanted=all on February 29, 2024.

Tavernise, S. (2016, February 12). *Disparity in life spans of the rich and the poor is growing.* Accessed at www.nytimes.com/2016/02/13/health/disparity-in-life-spans-of-the-rich-and-the-poor-is-growing.html on February 29, 2024.

World Economic Forum. (2020). *The future of jobs report 2020*. Accessed at www.weforum.org/publications/the-future-of-jobs-report-2020/in-full/infographics-e4e69e4de7 on February 15, 2024.

Alexander McNeece, PhD, is the director of instructional services and state and federal grants for Garden City School District in Garden City, Michigan. McNeece previously served as a high school football coach, elementary teacher, and middle school English language arts teacher. He is an active member of the Metro Bureau's Council of Academic Leadership in Michigan, where he has served as a state-level committee liaison. In 2017, with a team of teachers and principals, he presented to the Michigan State Board of Education based on the tremendous early literacy growth the district achieved with the PLC at Work process. As a consultant, McNeece has worked with districts around the United States and Canada to help close the achievement gap, transform school culture, strengthen the school-improvement process, and develop pedagogy to help students love learning.

He holds both a bachelor's and a master's degree in curriculum and instruction from Michigan State University. He earned a doctor of philosophy degree in educational leadership from Eastern Michigan University. He was an award-winning principal at Douglas Elementary School and has written multiple children's books. McNeece's professional books, *Launching and Consolidating Unstoppable Learning* and *Loving What They Learn,* help teachers develop strong instructional cultures in their classrooms.

To learn more about Alexander McNeece's work, visit www.alexandermcneece.com or follow @AlexMcNeece on X.

Charles Sheppard, MEd, is a former elementary and middle school principal and current middle school teacher in Maryland. He has always been dedicated to finding innovative ways to engage and inspire his students and staff.

Sheppard has a passion for education and is known for his ability to create positive and supportive learning environments through connections with the people around him. He has a strong belief in the power of education to change lives and is committed to helping all students reach their full potential. In his role as a teacher and principal, Sheppard has always focused on promoting student engagement and fostering a love of learning. He has been a positive voice for healthy school cultures from boardrooms to staff lounges.

He earned a bachelor's degree from the University of Delaware and a master's degree from Wilmington University.

To book Alexander McNeece or Charles Sheppard for professional development, contact pd@SolutionTree.com.

CHAPTER 2

Empowering Believers to Speak Up: The Fundamentalist Playbook

By Alexander McNeece and Charles Sheppard

As the cochair of her school's guiding coalition and a teacher with eight years of experience, Sarah felt a little defeated. The guiding coalition had been tasked to support student achievement. As the end of November approached, she was still encountering resistance from some of her colleagues regarding a new instructional practice that the team was trying to implement.

During the first month of school, the guiding coalition had found a research-based inventory to assess student engagement with their lessons. There was consensus across the school that student engagement was an issue. The results of the inventory came back, showing a need to address student feelings around mistakes and the existing sentiment that failures were not part of the learning process. The results were surprising but interesting, as the team had never had a conversation about engagement from that viewpoint. The inventory revealed that students needed classroom-level strategies that helped them process mistakes, enabled risk-taking, and increased conversation around the learning.

The guiding coalition delved into the research about growth mindset. They found a strategy with strong evidence of success: the implementation of cooperative learning. They found the research to back the initiative—classrooms that routinely use student collaboration create learning cultures where learning is a process, and positive struggle helps students learn even more deeply

(McNeece, 2019). The team decided on a path to change student outcomes. The principal, who also sat on the guiding coalition, agreed and was supportive.

At the next staff meeting, the teachers on the guiding coalition shared data, research, and even showcased the cooperative strategies. Staff gave feedback, and teachers who were already employing similar classroom strategies shared tips and possible pitfalls to avoid. All around the room, heads were nodding.

The following day, Sarah finished a typical morning of instruction and went to the staff lounge for lunch. Walking in, she noticed her colleagues immediately grew quiet. She purchased a soda and sat down with them. There was an uncomfortably long silence. The eyes of two of her colleagues seemed to lock onto the one in the middle, Tara, waiting for a comment to be made.

"I hope you don't take this the wrong way, but do you really think that having students work in groups is going to fix the fact that these parents don't care enough about their kids to help them with homework?" Tara said.

Sarah felt a sudden flash of anger. There were so many mischaracterizations in that statement. First, it diminished the amount of work the guiding coalition put into the plan. It dismissed the research they found and even misconstrued the cooperative learning strategies as work in groups. It ignored the obvious positive reaction of the collective group during the meeting. But what made Sarah the angriest was blaming the community's parents. Sarah was not under any illusion that parent involvement was ideal, but she had always found her students' parents supportive and wanting the best for their children.

Having just bitten into her sandwich, processing this blame-laden and dismissive comment, she wanted to say something but thought it was just *Tara being Tara*, so she didn't. Sarah felt defeated and she retreated, thinking it was better to save her energy for the students.

Sarah missed a chance—not just for a comeback, but for a response that could plant a seed and begin an ongoing conversation that would have helped Tara grow and ensured the other teachers at the table knew that the informal network of communication at that school was not going to be dominated by counterproductive talk.

We all probably have a story like this. These experiences strike at the core of our educational beliefs, yet just as in Sarah's case, they go unchallenged and embed themselves within school culture. They are the tactics of Fundamentalists, who Anthony Muhammad (2018) identifies as:

> Staff members who are not only opposed to change but organize to resist and thwart any change initiative. They can wield tremendous political power and are a major obstacle in implementing meaningful school reform. (p. 40)

For our students, we must remain grounded in our beliefs and help Fundamentalists through the changes necessary for students to be successful. If you are a change agent in your school, I'm sure you have experienced some type of resistance. It's the same story; the school has a problem to solve, some members of the school want to develop a change, and others resist that change.

Change agents have been unsuccessful for a multitude of reasons, but the key to overcoming problems is by making sure that we, the Believers, speak up. Anthony Muhammad (2018) defines Believers as:

> Educators who believe in the core values that make up a healthy school culture. They believe that all of their students are capable of learning and that they have a direct impact on student success. (p. 39)

Cultures become healthier when Believers' voices balance Fundamentalists' voices. This chapter breaks down the situations, analyzes resistors' motivations, and gives you the tools to have the important conversations that help your culture grow. Let's get into the Fundamentalist playbook this chapter presents, which includes knowing your school's communication networks, seeking to understand motivation, and speaking up.

Know Your School's Communication Networks

The first key concept is understanding your school's communication networks. A healthy school culture is one where "educators have an unwavering belief in the ability of all of their students to achieve success, and they pass that belief on to others in *overt* and *covert* ways" (Muhammad, 2018, p. 20). Every school has both a formal (overt) and informal (covert) communication network. This is an important distinction because, in many school cultures, the level of communicated belief in students' ability to be successful changes between what we say in our staff meetings to what is said in the staff lounge.

Formal

Your school's formal culture is the "party line" or what is officially said in staff meetings, emails, and committees. It's on posters and in your mission statement. Echoing the healthy school culture definition stated earlier, during these overt communications, it's typical to expect staff to communicate the belief that all students can learn. For example, many educators have a signature at the bottom of their emails. It includes the name of the sender and usually the school's mission statement or a motivational message about learning. You would never see an email signature that had the sender's name and the mantra, "If parents just helped with homework, these kids wouldn't be so far behind."

Can you imagine a superintendent or principal receiving a printed copy of a message home with that type of toxic comment? It would be on the evening news. Furthermore, teacher to teacher, the purveyor of the toxic comment would be shunned by peers. Yet comments like those are voiced in the informal network, and no such protest is the norm.

If your formal network routinely allows for toxic comments about students, learning, staff, leadership, parents, or the community, this is where you must begin as a staff. For example, if the principal says when opening the staff meeting, "I know you didn't read the chapter, but let's look at it anyway," the formal culture is communicating acceptance of the toxic norm of avoiding learning. Another example may be a staff member intentionally and routinely skipping a staff or collaborative team meeting without even an inquiry about their absence. Identify those comments or actions as extremely dangerous and work to change them immediately.

Informal

This informal communication culture is the web of interactions in the staff lounge, the parking lot, and text message groups. These are spaces that are much harsher in toxic cultures, where communication norms are sometimes extremely negative. These are the spaces where Believers have historically not spoken up. See figure 2.1 for a visual of a school's formal and informal communication culture locations.

The informal network is the underbelly of the communication culture. Collegiate professors and researchers Sandra I. Musanti and Lucretia Pence (2010) pose interesting points about the tradition of isolation in the American public school system and how that isolation forms strong peer-to-peer interactions. Our macro-culture of schools has developed to rely on the informal network—arguably more than the formal. While many positives exist in the informal network, the unchallenged negativity needs to be addressed.

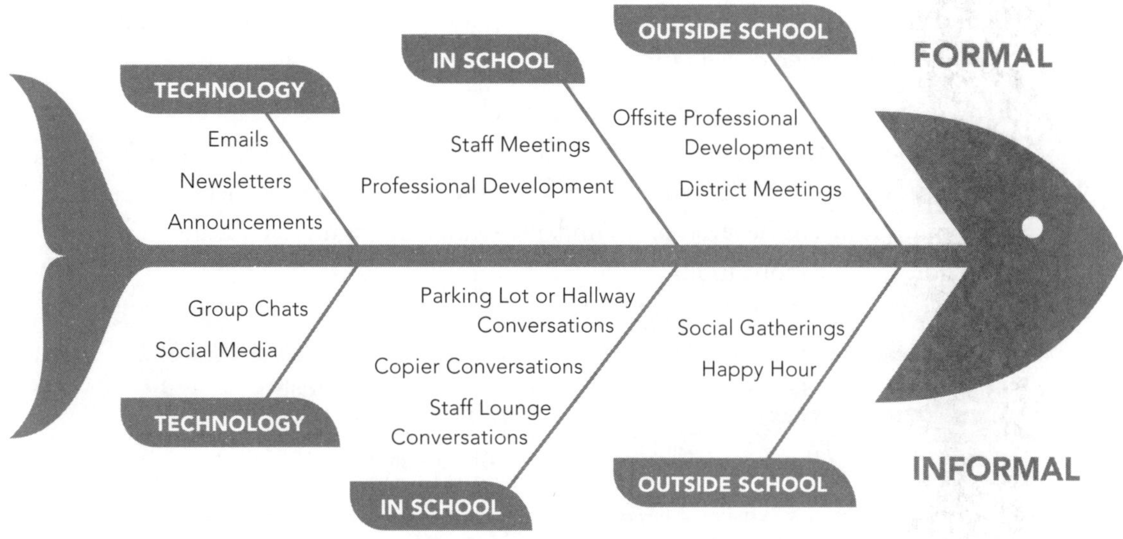

Figure 2.1: Schools' formal and informal communication culture locations.

This is the first aspect of the Fundamentalist's playbook to understand: we must have Believers and Fundamentalists exchange ideas in the informal network where the Believer is equipped with a proper frame of mind and a solid base of information to adjust in the critical moments to help the resistor think and reflect. This is not one conversation at one moment but multiple conversations that truly seek to engage those would-be resistors and help them join the team. We must make sure the voices of change agents are abundant and unapologetically a part of the informal communication network. If they aren't, let's get to work.

Seek to Understand Motivation

The Merriam-Webster dictionary defines a *playbook* as "a stock of usual tactics or methods" (Playbook, n.d.). These are used in sports, competition, or in other situations where we aim to succeed. These playbooks contain plans for offense and defense, and they are manifestations of our philosophies of success or survival. If you gain access to your competitor's playbook, you know their actions before they make them.

We suggest Believers do the exact same thing. By reverse engineering the reasons behind a Fundamentalist's behavior, we can preemptively identify how to respond and what help they need to grow. This is our opportunity to help

Fundamentalists. Believers must identify the motivations, break down the arguments, and provide consultation to overcome the resistance.

We developed this model from research to give you a perspective on Fundamentalists' thinking. Professor Richard R. Snyder (2017) did an excellent study about experienced teachers' resistance. His framework helps us see the motivations of Believers and Fundamentalists. See figure 2.2 for this connection and the motivations.

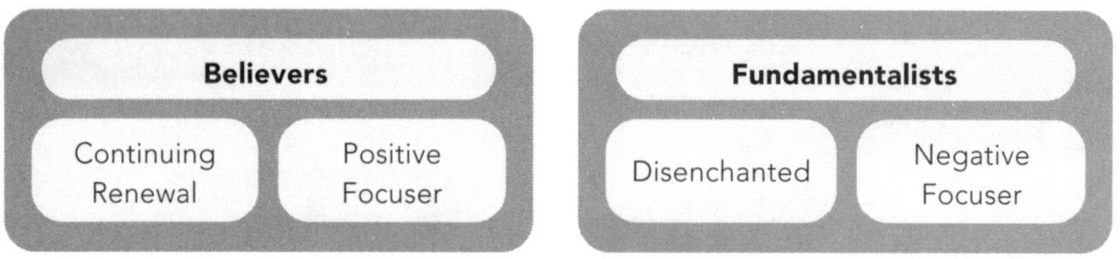

Source: Muhammad, 2018; Snyder, 2017.

Figure 2.2: Motivations of believers and fundamentalists.

The continuing renewal group are Believers with high levels of agency and self-efficacy. Harking back to the language of Muhammad's (2018) *Transforming School Culture*, these educators have the *will* (agency) and redevelop the *skill* (self-efficacy) to keep them at the top of their game. The positive focuser group are also veteran staff who do not fight change and help to develop it. With that said, these Believers also need support from their peers because a positive outlook will tarnish without supporting their agency and proper skills development (Muhammad, 2018).

To be clear, Believers with the motivation of continuing renewal or positive focus will resist change they feel is not in students' best interests (Muhammad, 2018; Snyder, 2017). For example, a veteran Believer could be called out for their lack of enforcement of the school's no hoodie policy. Is this Fundamentalist behavior or their adherence to a belief that best trauma-informed practices are to ignore the hood? Knowing your staff motivation is key, and some resistance is not inherently Fundamentalist behavior. We should expect continuing renewal and positive focusers to resist when a school adopts a one-size-fits-all policy that does not actually align with student learning.

Fundamentalists' motivations can be framed as disenchanted, or toxic, negative focusers. Disenchanted teachers may have been positive focusers who did not have the self-efficacy to improve or the support of the administration or a colleague. Their grievance originates from the system, as these teachers would have been part of previous failed change initiatives (Snyder, 2017). In our experience with disenchanted staff, they grow with the system's expectations when they see positive momentum for change and understand the logic of the change.

Negative focusers seem to have internalized their resistance. They make it personal. They will be the most negative in the informal network. These educators need your help, and you need to evaluate and understand their deepest motivations. These motivations, found in figure 2.3, unify multiple studies on teacher motivations and resistance.

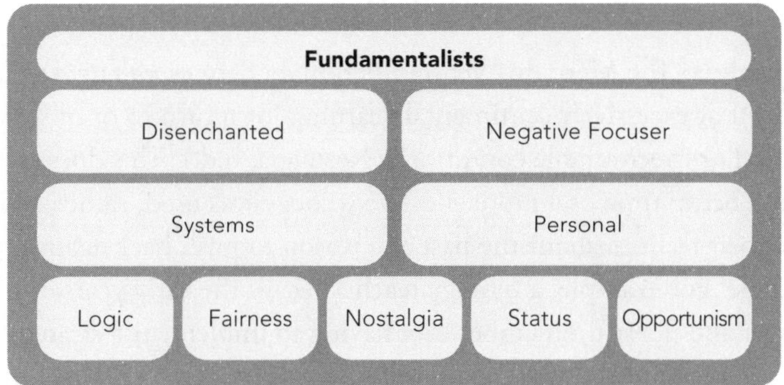

Source: Goodson et al., 2006, as cited in Snyder, 2017; Konakli & Akdeniz, 2022; Muhammad, 2018; Snyder, 2017; Sommers, 2021.

Figure 2.3: Motivations of fundamentalists.

The following are short explanations of each motivation and the type of resistance you would expect based on that motivation for a hypothetical schoolwide strategy where all teachers will include a writing component in their lessons to address low writing scores on the most recent state or provincial test.

- **Logic:** The change doesn't make sense to the teacher. Resistors don't see how it will benefit the students. Logical reasons for not adopting a new strategy should be addressed in the implementation plan. If the resistor's concerns are addressed during the change process, their concerns can be quickly mitigated. With that said, new concerns always appear as implementation begins; you should expect them. You can quickly help those logical resistors when their voices are heard. Not listening to developing logical issues will entrench Fundamentalists. An example is an art teacher who doesn't clearly see where in their lessons would be best to implement a short writing piece: "I just don't see the best time to implement this in my class."

- **Fairness:** This happens when a teacher feels the new policy, practice, or procedure is an undue burden to themselves or others. It has to do with perceptions of workload, breaking habits, and changes in what a teacher has grown comfortable with. An example of this is a mathematics teacher who doesn't think writing should have to be used in the classroom because of how much content there already is to cover. The teacher is challenged with implementing the change because they perceive that it doesn't fit in the current workload: "I would love to use writing in my class, but I have so many standards to cover."
- **Nostalgia:** The Merriam-Webster dictionary defines *nostalgia* as "a wistful or excessively sentimental yearning for return to or of some past period or irrecoverable condition" (Nostalgia, n.d.). This doesn't mean it was a better time or a more effective strategy was used; rather, resistors use their feelings about the past as a reason to push back against today's change. For example, a biology teacher recalls the early years of their career and doesn't remember ever having to implement a strategy like this: "We never did this before. I used to love teaching biology; they're ruining it!"
- **Status:** This deals with the interpersonal relationships and social status a teacher has in the building. Adopting a strategy could be problematic for a relationship if a vocal resistor is a close friend. It could also be politically challenging for a teacher to adopt a change if their status in the building could be upended. For example, the band teacher, who is also union president, sees value in focusing on writing but won't support the change as a small contingent of fellow staff members are voicing frustration, and the teacher doesn't want to appear weak: "This sounds like a good idea, but the teachers will never go for it."
- **Opportunism:** These resistors are willing to push back against change they know is needed to gain a personal benefit, sacrificing the well-being of the students for their own self-interest. Moving classrooms, being named a department chair, or adjusting the master schedule to fit their wants are all examples of a resistor holding change hostage for personal reasons. For example, the physical education teacher thinks the requirement to include a writing component in lessons makes sense and would be easily adopted through a strategy like an exit ticket, but

> the teacher resists. The teacher always wanted an extra prep period and the title of department chair. Behind closed doors, the teacher voices support for the change and will get the rest of the department to follow suit if the administration names them department chair: "Without a new department chair, I don't see this being successful."

Humans are complex, and the goal of this framework is to help you think about the resistor's reasons and begin a conversation to help your school grow together. Fundamentalists can have primary and secondary issues when resisting a change, and your understanding of their motives will grow as conversations continue. This model is a starting point to help you, but we have encountered situations where the motivations of the negative focuser seemed to be staunchly affixed just to a negative outlook. The next section will help you break those walls down.

Speak Up!

It's time to act once we know the space and are empowered with the concepts of motivation. To help prepare you for this, we suggest a three-part cycle as you and your team of Believers cultivate a foothold in the informal communication network: plan, talk, and reflect.

Plan

Plan for a conversation first. Identify the Fundamentalist's foundational motivations that might be threatened by the proposed change (Snyder, 2017). It's important to remember to honestly try to see the other person's point of view and be empathetic to their mindset (Carnegie, 2009). This does not mean you will believe they are correct in their resistance, but if you can understand it, you can plan responses that help them overcome their negative motivation. Does the resistor have a systems focus or a personal focus? After that, which of the five underlying motivations may be the main driver of their resistance?

If you identify a disenchanted, systems-level resistor, it's helpful to plan how to share your own feelings around those motivations and how they have changed. Consider using the three Fs approach (Sommers, 2021).

1. "I **felt** . . ."
2. "But now I **feel** . . ."
3. "Because I **found** out . . ."

Plan a statement you can make during the conversation that follows your logic of personal growth. This helps you connect your own thinking to theirs, express how you grew, and give the reason why you grew. Figure 2.4 shows how to use the three Fs with a resistor.

Topic	Disenchanted Resistor Statement	Three Fs Response
Collaborative Teams	(Logic) "Making us all sit in a room for sixty minutes keeps us from getting the real work done."	"I felt confused when we started team collaboration. Now I feel it's my favorite time of the day because I found my team talks about what I need every day—sometimes it's planning a lesson together, building the assessment, or even looking at the data. Everything we do there helps me have better days. I don't feel alone anymore."
Common Assessments	(Fairness) "We have too many common assessments to give!"	"I felt we were assessing too often and it was taking time away from instruction. Now I feel common assessments save me time because I found out how we use the data, and I have improved my instruction methods after hearing from my team about the strategies they used to teach those concepts where I wasn't excelling."
Curriculum	(Nostalgia) "Our students were better with the old series we had when I first started in the building. This curriculum doesn't work."	"I felt that way when we started using it. Now I feel like it's much better because I found I can see how engaged the students are with the instructional strategies."

Figure 2.4: Disenchanted staff and the three Fs response.

This is one of the first playbook elements in the informal network to help flip your Fundamentalist. Disenchanted staff need to see a different path. Use the three Fs to insert transformative ideas into the informal network.

Unfortunately, negative focusers will not respond the same to the three Fs as their resistor counterparts. Believers need to know that negative focusers' language in these types of conversations is usually negative and circular (Olitsky, 2021). Be ready for any or all other motivations to be used as cover when you cut their initial circular thinking. The negative-focuser Fundamentalist will have multiple layers of defenses while you drill down to the core that they don't want to change.

See this circular conversation between two teachers, where teacher A doesn't want to adopt a new strategy, and teacher B is trying unsuccessfully to help her colleague grow.

> ***Teacher A:*** "I really don't see the point in trying out this new teaching strategy that the school is pushing. It's just not my style, you know?"
>
> ***Teacher B:*** "But if it can benefit the students and aligns with the school's goals, isn't it worth trying something new?"
>
> ***Teacher A:*** "Well, it's not just about my style. I think it's too time-consuming. I already have a lot on my plate."
>
> ***Teacher B:*** "I understand time is a concern, but the school believes it's crucial. Perhaps it gets more efficient with practice?"
>
> ***Teacher A:*** "It's not just about time; it's also about the resources. I don't think we have the right materials for this strategy."

The Fundamentalist's verbal defense consists of comebacks that assume the same argument by adding new elements each round to defend their reason to not change. We advise Believers not to engage in this merry-go-round of thinking and instead, upon realizing they are in this cycle, change tactics to simply say a variation of, "Go on, tell me more, what else?" (Sinek, 2021). Be prepared to use this powerful tool for de-escalation. It pushes the Fundamentalist to jump into the thinking part of their brain while helping you avoid continually triggering them emotionally through a combative back-and-forth exchange.

This is a critical moment, when the Fundamentalist has exhausted their list of perceived barriers, and now there is room for you to ask questions, show you listened, and engage in dialogue to promote growth. Use the strategies in the next section to help you have a productive conversation in the moment.

Talk

Conversation is key for reversing resistant behavior (Snyder, 2017). These conversations could happen anywhere in the informal network. We all want to be better in the moments when these important conversations take place. There are multiple strategies that you can employ to help you in this verbal exchange (adapted from Carnegie, 2009).

- Start positively and keep a friendly or professional demeanor. It can greatly benefit the interaction now and next time.
- Don't be drawn into a situation where both parties may feel emotionally triggered. Stay calm and remember you're in this for the long haul. Consider this as a collaborative process.
- Demonstrate respect for your colleague's viewpoints by giving them ample time to express their thoughts. Try to avoid cutting the other teacher off mid-sentence.
- Instead of saying, "You're wrong," try to find common ground and encourage agreement. Engage the other person by prompting them to say "yes" early in the conversation about philosophical elements where you find agreement.
- Allow your colleague to contribute significantly to the discussion; make it a dialogue rather than a one-sided conversation. Adults learn through talking, so make sure to ask questions that help them drill down to the actual source of the problem.
- Appeal to the higher, noble motives to guide the conversation in a positive direction. Every teacher began this profession as a calling. Look for ways to reconnect the change with those positive foundations.

Reflect

After the conversation, consider taking a few notes to help you think about the next steps. No matter how surprising or frustrating an event has been, reflection can help all of us learn from today to help plan for a better tomorrow (Bailey & Rehman, 2022). Even our failures, like a conversation with a Fundamentalist that didn't go as planned, can become tomorrow's success through personal analysis. We suggest giving yourself some processing time to think about what was said. The puzzle of human motivations is not solved quickly, and you will also probably have some strong emotions from the conversation.

Plan your collaborative, supportive follow-up. This is not about being right; it's about supporting your teammates and developing a healthy school culture that grows to meet students' needs. Know that, regardless of the outcome, the philosophical debate entering into the informal communication network is a win for your school, the students, and—believe it or not—that teacher. The win is in the process.

Conclusion

In their book *Crucial Influence: Leadership Skills to Create Lasting Behavior Change*, best-selling authors Joseph Grenny and colleagues (2023) talk about the social power we have to change people. One person speaking up can influence an entire group. The authors prompt us to ask if the Believers have organized and recruited in the informal network to help accomplish their goals of all students learning. It's a provocative question because it's so much outside of our traditional norms, where the Believers are weak in the informal network (Muhammad, 2018). In short, we need Believers to act as Influencers by knowing the locations, motivations, and methods where we need their voices. Let's go back to the opening vignette when Sarah was confronted by Tara and what could have gone differently.

Recall what Tara said: "These parents don't care enough about their kids to help them with homework once in a while." While Tara is obviously playing on a frustration that many teachers have, it does not release us from the responsibility to continue innovating to help parents engage with their children's work. For example, Sarah's response could have been, "I know we all have challenges engaging the parents sometimes, but the strategy we are talking about, cooperative learning, has nothing to do with the parents. Using this strategy helps kids, especially those who don't have that support at home. But you are right, in addition to using great classroom strategies, we need to talk about increasing parent support. I'll take this to our next guiding coalition meeting."

If Tara attempts to use circular thinking, Sarah can adjust tactics and say, "What else is in *your* way of implementing cooperative learning?"

Drawing out as much from Tara as she can, and once there is space in the room, Sarah asks, "Is it true that you do recognize the issue with students and their engagement?"

Tara nods. Sarah has found a source of agreement, and she continues, "And it's important to all be on the same page, right?" Tara gives another positive affirmation. "Cooperative learning is what we have control over to increase engagement, and we have so many teachers in the building already using it well with great results, but all of the things you talked about are important, and I will be bringing them to the guiding coalition to get you the support you need."

The circular thinking is broken. Negativity starts to wane. More work will need to be done, but if Sarah genuinely follows up with Tara, the chances of her implementing cooperative learning skyrocket.

Believers will not have an outcome like this every time, but being part of these conversations is a healthy culture-developing activity. Consider the two other teachers in the room who have now had the chance to hear a Believer push back and share positive solutions to the real problems they face. They are now far more likely to implement change than if Fundamentalist thinking had triumphed. That is truly the point: silence can suggest acceptance. When you speak up, you change the culture. Use this new understanding of the Fundamentalist playbook to help your colleagues and school culture grow.

References and Resources

Bailey, J. R., & Rehman, S. (2022, March 4). *Don't underestimate the power of self-reflection.* Accessed at https://hbr.org/2022/03/dont-underestimate-the-power-of-self-reflection on April 25, 2024.

Carnegie, D. (2009). *How to win friends and influence people: Updated for the next generation of leaders.* New York: Simon & Schuster.

Cromwell, S. (2002). *Is your school culture toxic or positive?* Accessed at www.educationworld.com/a_admin/admin/admin275.shtml on September 10, 2024.

Goodson, I., Moore, S., & Hargreaves, A. (2006). Teacher nostalgia and the sustainability of reform: The generation and degeneration of teachers' missions, memory and meaning. *Educational Administration Quarterly, 42*(1), 42–61.

Grenny, J., Patterson, K., Maxfield, D., McMillan, R., & Switzler, A. (2023). *Crucial influence: Leadership skills to create lasting behavior change* (3rd ed.). New York: McGraw-Hill Education.

Konakli, T., & Akdeniz, R. (2022). The emergence, reasons, and results of resistance to change in teachers. *International Journal on Lifelong Education and Leadership, 8*(1). https://doi.org/10.25233/ijlel.1107137

McNeece, A. (2019). *Loving what they learn: Research-based strategies to increase student engagement.* Bloomington, IN: Solution Tree Press.

Muhammad, A. (2018) *Transforming school culture: how to overcome staff division* (2nd ed.). Bloomington, IN: Solution Tree Press.

Musanti, S. I., & Pence, L. (2010). Collaboration and teacher development: Unpacking resistance, constructing knowledge, and navigating identities. *Teacher Education Quarterly, 37*(1), 73–89.

Nostalgia. (n.d.). In *Merriam-Webster's online dictionary.* Accessed at www.merriam-webster.com/dictionary/nostalgia on September 18, 2024.

Olitsky, S. (2021). Identity, agency, and the internal conversations of science and math teachers implementing instructional reforms in high-need urban schools. *Cultural Studies of Science Education, 16*, 19–45. https://doi.org/10.1007/s11422-019-09965-4

Playbook. (n.d.). In *Merriam-Webster's online dictionary*. Accessed at www.merriam-webster.com/dictionary/playbook on September 18, 2024.

Sinek, S. (2021, November 5). *The art of listening*. Accessed at https://awakeuniversity.maincross.org/public-personas/5660/article/2380/the-art-of-listening-simon-sinek on April 25, 2024.

Snyder, R. R. (2017). Resistance to change among veteran teachers: Providing voice for more effective engagement. *International Journal of Educational Leadership Preparation, 12*(1), 1–14.

Sommers, W. A. (2020). *Responding to resistance: Thirty strategies to manage conflict in your school*. Bloomington, IN: Solution Tree Press.

Carlos Johnson is a professional speaker, trainer, author, and school administrator. For roughly twenty years, he has consulted, trained, and held seats on public, charter, and private school boards. Along with his team of consultants at IMAGE of Success, "Coach Carlos" uses many of Anthony Muhammad's (2018) philosophies from *Transforming School Culture: How to Overcome Staff Division*. He has successfully turned around three failing schools simply by concentrating on the school's culture and the school-home relationship. His particular focus is on the idea that instructional teams are more than just the delivery system for high-quality instruction. Their relationships with students and families can also drive or destroy school culture and performance. The research and results from this philosophy led him to create his systematic approach to building healthy performance-based relationships with all stakeholders. He calls this system PowerEngage. He is the author of *Power Engage: Seven Power Moves for Building Strong Relationships to Increase Engagement With Students and Parents*.

In addition to working with district leaders and instructional teams, Coach Carlos's online parent training at www.PowerParentingU.com helps hundreds of parents each year become certified Partner Parents by training them on what he calls the seven meaningful minimum strategies for engaging with their child's school. As head of school, he led the Male Leadership Academy in Charlotte, North Carolina, to consistent enrollment increases, and his parental promise of at least one year's growth for one year's attendance was met each year for 100 percent of his students.

To learn more about Carlos Johnson's work, visit www.imageofsuccess.com.

To book Carlos Johnson for professional development, contact pd@SolutionTree.com.

CHAPTER 3

Doing Is Learning: The Power of Project-Based Learning

By Carlos Johnson

While I did not know it then, I was introduced to project-based learning as a young man when my mother turned a routine grocery shopping trip into a captivating lesson. As my sister and I strolled through the supermarket aisles, we weren't just filling our cart with essentials; we were also embarking on a hands-on exploration of various subjects. My mother had carefully crafted a project that engaged our minds and ignited our curiosity. Our mission was to plan and prepare a family dinner from scratch, with each member assigned a specific role. The grocery store became our classroom, and the shopping list transformed into a dynamic project outline.

Mathematics came alive as my mother demanded we compare prices, calculate discounts, and estimate the total cost of chosen groceries. Turning the produce section into a science lab, she explained the nutritional benefits of different fruits and vegetables. The bakery aisle became a language arts workshop as we read and discussed the origin and ingredients of various bread types.

The project extended beyond the store. Back home, my sister took charge of writing a step-by-step recipe, enhancing her language skills. Armed with a newfound understanding of measurements, I confidently helped my mother measure ingredients. The dinner table transformed into a collaborative workspace where we shared stories and laughter while preparing the meal.

What started as a grocery shopping trip evolved into a dynamic project that touched on multiple subjects and life skills. Our family didn't just bring home groceries—we brought home a profound appreciation for learning through real-world experiences.

This story showcases how a simple trip to the market can become a rich project-based learning opportunity where education seamlessly integrates into everyday life. My mother empowered us to see the world as our classroom, turning the mundane into the extraordinary through innovative teaching moments.

In my work in education, I have tried to develop experiences that, like my family's trip to the grocery store, integrate education into everyday life that benefits students and contributes to a healthy school culture. Research indicates that a positive school climate is closely associated with increased student engagement, improved academic performance, and enhanced social-emotional development (Bradshaw et al., 2015). Furthermore, engaged students are more likely to exhibit prosocial behaviors, reducing disruptive incidents and creating a more conducive learning environment (Bradshaw et al., 2018).

A highly engaged classroom is crucial to developing a healthy school culture. This chapter explores how project-based learning can help schools shift from a teacher- to a learner-centered approach to improve student engagement and school culture.

From a Teacher- to a Learner-Centered Approach

Professional teacher training programs seek to equip student teachers with pedagogical skills to aid them in their quest to impart knowledge to learners. Although these various teaching methods are broadly categorized as teacher-based and learner-based, the reality is most schools practice a teacher-centered approach, which is convenient for the teachers and, as you would guess, not for the learner. Studies show that teacher-centered methods can be particularly effective in subjects requiring the transmission of factual knowledge and foundational skills (Bell, 2010; Murphy, Eduljee, & Croteau, 2021). This approach is valuable for its clarity, organization, and ability to maintain classroom order and academic rigor (Bell, 2010).

In taking a teacher-centered approach, teachers may, at the end of an academic season, proudly report to the relevant stakeholders that the syllabus for the year is finished; in reality, however, only the teacher covered the syllabus while the learners were left far behind. The teacher-centered approach, despite its traditional roots, comes with several disadvantages that can hinder the overall educational experience. One significant drawback is that it fosters a dependency on the teacher, limiting students' ability to develop self-directed learning skills essential for lifelong learning (Kompa, 2013). Additionally, students who can't keep up with the teacher and have not developed self-directed learning skills can easily be left behind. This teaching approach is successful insofar as it produces a room filled with disengaged students. Teachers grapple with the demands of set timelines and standardized tests students must pass with flying colors. Learners struggle to make sense of this burdensome ritual of cramming or memorizing notes in readiness for exams in addition to dealing with challenges such as social acceptance and family issues.

Project-based learning—an instructional approach designed to provide opportunities for students to develop knowledge and skills through engaging projects about challenges they may face in the real world (PowerSchool, 2021)—is an engine that can drive student engagement so learners can experience the real power of education.

Teachers and students are no longer handcuffed to traditional learning experiences with project-based learning. The spirit behind project-based learning is the authentic experiences students get when they successfully complete projects, like organizing an event or making a presentation. Project-based learning involves creativity and critical thinking that prepares students to tackle whatever challenges come their way, both in the classroom and beyond. We live in a project-based world; this approach to learning lets students know that their learning is not just disconnected theory but based in real-world applications. Students can then appreciate that they are being positioned to tackle both present and future problems by processing and implementing solutions. This approach to teaching and learning is ideal as it aligns with motivation expert Daniel Pink's (2009) view that autonomy, mastery, and purpose are the three things that intrinsically motivate people.

The Benefits of Project-Based Learning

Researchers Samira F. Al-Khrisha and Othman N. Mansour (2021) note that students improve their critical-thinking skills through the various stages of implementing project-based assignments. Critical thinking requires that someone can analyze and evaluate a matter and proceed to make a reasonable judgment. Project-based learning, therefore, invites students to look at arguments, make observations, review available evidence and facts, and use them to make informed interpretations. These are skills that will serve students well in the real world of work, postsecondary education, and life in general.

Al-Khrisha and Mansour (2021) further affirm that project-based learning promotes a positive, structured environment conducive to student-teacher dialogue. Instead of having teachers and students on two opposing sides, project-based learning puts both teachers and students on one side—the winning side. This is more so because, in addition to working with their fellow students and individually reflecting on their work, students must also be under the mentorship and guidance of the teacher, whom they must consult periodically (Roeser, Eccles, & Sameroff, 2000). This is not because the knowledge they gain is abstract, but rather because students view teachers as partners in problem solving in the learning process, adding value for students and to the world around them (Allen et al., 2013).

Project-based learning motivates and encourages students, a move that significantly catalyzes student engagement (Almulla, 2020). It is widely accepted within education circles that motivation is a critical prerequisite for student involvement in learning activities. Motivation is therefore rightly considered to be the catalyst for any kind of learning, and student motivation revolves around the belief that whatever project students work on will go a long way toward completing demanding tasks, as well as activities that appeal to their interests, motives, and personal needs (Gallagher, 2015).

As students participate in their projects and collaborate with their team members and teachers, they have a personal reason to be physically present in school, motivated by the fact that they are not coming to be lectured but to work on something they enjoy (Cervantes, Hemmer, & Kouzekanani, 2015; Lynch, 2022). Project-based learning can be seen as an important element in keeping students coming back to school. Chronic absenteeism, for example, becomes a thing of the past with project-based learning. Students with chronic absenteeism usually have problems with both reading and writing and feel out of touch socially and emotionally (Anderson, 2022; Nachshon & Horowitz-Kraus, 2019). This feeling of academic insufficiency and disconnect pushes them farther and farther away from school. Project-based learning makes room for both physical and social engagement in group work, thus creating a comfortable environment of peer relationships for otherwise shy and uncertain learners (Lynch, 2022). Chronically absent students can view physical creations in project-based learning upon returning to school, during which time they can actively participate in discussions and make inquiries, subsequently becoming able to visualize what others accomplished in their absence.

The benefit of project-based learning for teachers is that, instead of just firing standardized questions at students or providing set-in-stone instructions, teachers have freedom and flexibility to ask research questions about real-life situations guided by their own experiences or observations. For example, a teacher could provide prompts to students organized into groups that are each tasked with a unique project. Since teachers are not at the center of instruction in project-based learning, they have the flexibility to observe student learning and multiple opportunities for assessment as students work both in groups and independently demonstrate their capabilities.

Project-based learning products are not necessarily an end in themselves; these projects may require products or findings be presented to communities. For instance, in a science class, students might take on projects about nature preservation, community gardens, or clean water. In mathematics, they could do a project on fundraising for a community nonprofit. In English language arts, they could tackle a project designing advertising for community outreach. Students in a social studies class could pick a topic for civic outreach, encourage historic preservation, or even suggest community planning. In the words of Rushton Hurley, "If students are sharing their work with the world, they want it to be good. If they are just sharing it with you, they just want it to be good enough" (Ralf, 2016). Project-based learning nurtures a culture of excellence, both in school and outside of school, where students may feel compelled to seek solutions in their futures to more complex global problems.

According to Carla M. Evans (2019), an associate at the National Center for the Improvement of Educational Assessment, students taking part in project-based learning are at an advantage to improve scientific practices like formulating questions, planning and conducting investigations, and analyzing data. These research skills become the cornerstone of solving real-life challenges and keeping students engaged. Market research and analysis are common skills needed in business, as entrepreneurs seek to penetrate new markets and claim a firm grip on existing markets. Students who already have these skills will have an advantage. Beyond business, students who wish to venture into professional training in areas such as criminal justice or investigative journalism benefit from exposure to project-based learning, as well as those who may go into politics and government and are looking to offer solutions to the citizens they serve. It is also worth noting that data analysis is an area of interest for many young people. Learners can access platforms like www.theforage.com or https://data.gov to analyze various data sets on topics of interest like transportation, health, education, or climate change. Students engaging in data analysis during project-based learning are positioned for meaningful engagements in life beyond the classroom walls.

Students engaged in project-based learning can transfer the skills they acquire by applying them to personal challenges they may encounter in life. Projects often require group members to step back and reflect on problems versus solutions (De La Paz & Hernández-Ramos, 2013); adapt to new challenges, including in interpersonal relationships (Prensky, 2014); take risks by sharing individual opinions and communicating (Bell, 2010); and collaborating with others (Fullan & Scott, 2014). Because students will have a point of reference from their projects in school, they can confidently say, "This challenge seems familiar; we have been there, and if we did it before, we can do it again!" This outcome is a particularly rewarding part of project-based learning. One study on transference of project-based learning skills shows that graduate students doing clinical work increased their thinking before, during, and after the project; enhanced their communication with patients; had more effective communication with colleagues; and improved their proactivity (Stanton, Guerin, & Barrett, 2017).

Perhaps the greatest evidence of the shortcomings of many traditional instructional approaches is the frustration many graduates feel when seeking employment in a market that prefers those with varied skill sets rather than those with heaps of academic accomplishments but few or no skills in real-world problem solving. Employers are concerned with what a potential candidate can do and how they can critically think. The World Economic Forum (2020) reports that the right skills will take precedence over academic qualifications of college graduates.

It is worth noting that in most colleges or technical colleges, students are quite engaged with hands-on assignments, which, in the end, makes them more preferred in the job market. Individuals who have acquired vocational training in colleges or technical colleges stand a better chance of landing first jobs compared to individuals with general education (Verhaest et al., 2018, as cited in Forster et al., 2018). Suppose for a moment that K–12 schools implemented project-based learning from elementary through high school. Wouldn't this approach produce a formidable working force for addressing real-world problems? Who knows, maybe we would not be struggling with formulating climate change policies and legislations that people do not quite embrace, as solving real problems would be seen as expected, everyday work for everyone.

Using project-based learning with global issues like healthcare, pollution, and pandemics could propel young scholars into scientific careers where they will draw satisfaction from offering solutions to real-life, relevant problems that directly affect humanity (Wang, 2022).

Project-Based Learning and School Culture

Project-based learning is an equalizer that promotes inclusivity for students of all abilities, allowing them to produce meaningful projects and become the beneficiaries of knowledge. In a study on student perceptions of project-based learning in inclusive high school language arts classes, most students with disabilities, and those without, identify positively with project-based learning and so do their teachers (Boardman & Hovland, 2022). Students feel a sense of independence and connect their learning to their world. Students appreciate themselves and their cultural experiences because project-based learning recognizes and appreciates contributions by diverse groups. Project-based learning contributes to a sense of belonging because everyone has a role in the project. Learners who may have various challenges understand that it is not their speed or skill that matters as much as their engagement in the task and contribution to the project.

Project-based learning is a balanced instructional approach. In addition to improving technical skills, researchers Siti K. Ummah, Akhsanul In'am, and Rizal D. Azmi (2019) suggest that it promotes creativity and social skills. Research finds that student performance is improved with project-based learning. For example, researchers Inéz Ruiz-Rosa, Desiderio Gutiérrez-Taño, and Francisco J. Garcia-Rodríguez (2021) find that project-based learning activities for grade 5 learners improved their performance in science, although it did not necessarily overhaul their attitude toward the subject.

In schools, projects are traditionally reserved for certain subjects, like science. Likewise, it would be almost unimaginable for some subjects, like English language arts, to engage in projects. Project-based learning should not be reserved for certain subjects or courses; rather, it is an approach that can be applied in every discipline, as a single entity or by way of collaboration between subjects. The power of project-based learning is also not just for student populations from certain incomes; it can be utilized in every school. In many ways, project-based learning is the great equalizer.

While countries like Finland and Japan are known for being exemplary educationally, we can learn from African countries, like Kenya, Tanzania, Zimbabwe,

Zambia, Mozambique, Rwanda, and South Africa, that have embraced competency-based curriculum (Ruth & Ramadas, 2019). The UNESCO International Bureau of Education (2017) defines competency-based curriculum as an education system where emphasis is put on what learners can do and not what they know, focusing on identifying the diverse potential brought by every learner to the classroom, and nurturing their potential through different pathways. Project-based learning is at the heart of a competency-based curriculum—where both parents and teachers become collaborators with the learner, guiding them through various school projects. Rather than giving students a lot of written tests, learners are given projects that are assessed at every level, from conception of ideas and implementation to the project's conclusion.

Project-Based Learning in Action

I personally experienced the power and benefits of project-based learning when at the Male Leadership Academy in the Long Beach Unified School District in California, where many of our students were failing English language arts. As a school leader, I knew intimately that my instructional team was exhausted and close to burnout. At our next leadership meeting, we asked ourselves one question that changed everything for us: "What would our students like to do?" The power of that question is not in the answer—rather, it's in the last word of the question: *do*. We didn't ask ourselves, "What would they like to learn?" because that question would put the focus on our instructional team and what they would teach. We homed in on the verb *do*. Once that light bulb came on, we took off, setting out to improve our literacy scores. We departed from our traditional methodology and embraced project-based learning. One project had students investigating both local and international news on a variety of topics. The teams of students would write a news report at the end of every project. That is how the Male Leadership Academy News broadcast—a bi-monthly news program operated by students—was born.

Teams of students would then rehearse their news reports for presentation in front of a camera in a makeshift newsroom. Our partner, Johnson C. Smith, edited the broadcast. Students would then upload their news reports to the academy's YouTube page where parents and community partners, both key pillars of our project-based learning model, were always excited to view them. This example of project-based learning developed student literacy skills while expanding students' views beyond the classroom in a rich, multidisciplinary way. Authors Jal Mehta and Sarah Fine (2019), who have written extensively about deeper learning, acknowledge that it is not easy to define but generally involves learning that "moves beyond rote learning and shallow testing" (p. 10).

Creating a public newscast also invites students to meaningfully reflect on the quality of their research, writing, and presentation. In addition, the real-world broadcasting task also provided some unforeseen obstacles that students and teachers had to work through creatively, such as technical issues, giving students further opportunities to solve real-world problems.

An additional challenge in project-based learning that we encountered was finding enough roles to keep all students engaged. For instance, some students, like many adults, did not want to be in front of the camera. These students did not receive zeros, of course. Students took on roles that appealed to them and specialized in certain areas. Later, they expanded their knowledge by rotating roles and teaching each other what they learned while in the position, which helped build a sense of teamwork. The broadcast project can be used for classrooms of ten students or thirty. Support materials include sample project maps and lesson plans for developing topics, researching, and editing the work as recommended by Dana Gaertner (2021).

Male Leadership Academy News raised our literacy scores and encouraged our scholars to raise the standard of their expectations in every assignment and task. This project-based learning also had an uplifting effect on the staff's belief in students, and as Muhammad (2018) states:

> Students will learn more and be more successful in an environment where all educators *believe* they can learn at high levels and those educators work together to convince the students that they can achieve lofty academic goals teachers set for them. (p. 25)

Project-based learning can also involve visual and performing arts. For example, in one high school, students perform songs other students have written, reaching out to the community to raise funds for studio recording (Ryerse & Liebtag, 2018). Once recorded, the students work together again to launch their music, and then move forward with courage to market and sell their musical production. The students' school principal is involved in the project, and teachers take part in the production from beginning to end. This project illustrates the multidisciplinary approach project-based learning can take.

Another example of a multidisciplinary project is a mock election that engages learners in researching election practices and malpractices, drawing conclusions, and reporting their findings to the class or school community. Students use the concepts and skills from various disciplines, including mathematics for tallying votes, language for reading and writing details of voting materials and election processes, creative arts for preparing the voting materials, social studies or civic education for researching and understanding electoral laws, and even religious studies for advancing moral values like integrity and honesty, which are critical in elections. Table 3.1 provides some examples of possible projects for various subjects and grade levels from the book *Implementing Project-Based Learning* (Boss, 2015).

Table 3.1: Potential Projects

Potential Projects	Disciplines	Potential Approaches
Entrepreneurship and innovation projects	Science, technology, social studies, mathematics	Students use their creativity to produce solutions to real-world challenges, like using business strategies to address social or environmental problems in a classroom version of the popular reality television show *Shark Tank*. Students start with a problem, create an innovation, develop, market, and pitch their product.
Storytelling projects	English, technology, social studies, history	Students use storytelling to create content about subjects as an advocacy tool. For example, students might create comics or graphic novels about saving endangered species, plan and host poetry slams featuring their work, and screen their own multimedia creations during red-carpet events they have planned.
Geospatial projects	Geography, technology, science, English	Students collect, analyze, and present geographic data to address real issues in their community, such as determining the best location for offshore wind farms, investigating pollution prevalence in rural areas, or even recommending the best location for a new NFL franchise.
Data-literacy projects	Mathematics, civics, social studies, technology, English	Students become data literate by posing questions, analyzing information, and supporting their conclusions with reliable evidence. In data-literacy projects, students might research and analyze how a government collects information from its citizens and then determine a plan to reach every American around areas of importance to students, like social justice themes.
Media-literacy projects	English, technology, health and wellness, social studies	Students can both analyze and create multimedia content. They can analyze how media messages aim to influence their behavior, how media portrayals affect how they see themselves, and then use these as starting points to produce their own content, including podcasts and short films. They might analyze political messages and then create their own campaign ads or create a podcast about how to use social media to amplify youth voices in politics.

Conclusion

Project-based learning offers a perfect opportunity for connecting students to the world beyond their classroom, preparing them to accept and navigate the real-world challenges they will experience. Whereas memorization and regurgitation are short-term tactics for learning, project-based learning takes content engagement to a higher level and focuses on long-term retention and helping students develop a more positive attitude toward learning.

Educators might have some initial reservations about project-based learning, wondering if they have the time and training to implement it in the classroom (Kwietniewski, 2017). There has also been concern about the effectiveness of evaluating projects, especially when students use technology (Efstratia, 2014). Others might believe the amount of responsibility on students may be cumbersome. Some teachers may feel uncomfortable losing the control they have of the classroom with traditional teacher-centered instruction. I hope this chapter with its exploration of the student benefits of project-based learning makes clear that the possibilities—particularly cultivation of a positive school culture where students reflect on problems, create innovative solutions, and collaborate with group members (Zhang & Ma, 2023)—outweigh the reservations.

References and Resources

Allen, J., Gregory, A., Mikami, A., Lun, J., Hamre, B., & Pianta, R. (2013). Observations of effective teacher-student interactions in secondary school classrooms: Predicting student achievement with the classroom assessment scoring system—Secondary. *School Psychology Review, 42*(1), 76–98.

Al-Khrisha, S. F., & Mansour, O. N. (2021). The impact of teaching vocational education using project-based learning strategy on developing critical thinking skills among 10th grade students. *Ilkogretim Online, 20*(1), 1282–1296.

Almulla, M. A. (2020). The effectiveness of the project-based learning (PBL) approach as a way to engage students in learning. *Sage Open, 10*(3).

Anderson, J. (2019, May 1). *In search of deeper learning.* Accessed at www.gse.harvard.edu/ideas/edcast/19/05/search-deeper-learning on April 25, 2024.

Anderson, K. N. (2022). *Absenteeism: Crisis for students struggling to read* [Master's thesis, California State University, San Marcos]. ScholarWorks. https://scholarworks.calstate.edu/downloads/9z903531q.

Bell, S. (2010). Project-based learning for the 21st century: Skills for the future. *The Clearing House, 83*(2), 39–43.

Boardman, A. G, & Hovland, J. B. (2022). Student perceptions of project-based learning in inclusive high school language arts. *International Journal of Inclusive Education, 28*(10), 2235–2250.

Bradshaw, C. P., Pas, E. T., Debnam, K. J., & Johnson, S. L. (2015). A focus on implementation of Positive Behavioral Interventions and Supports (PBIS) in high schools: Associations with bullying and other indicators of school disorder. *School Psychology Review, 44*(4), 480–498.

Bradshaw, C. P., Pas, E. T., Bottiani, J. H., Debnam, K. J., Reinke, W. M., Herman, K. C., & Rosenberg, M. S. (2018). Promoting cultural responsivity and student engagement through Double Check coaching of classroom teachers: An efficacy study. *School Psychology Review, 47*(2), 118–134.

Boss, S. (2015). *Implementing project-based learning.* Bloomington, IN: Solution Tree Press.

Cervantes, B., Hemmer, L., & Kouzekanani, K. (2015). The impact of project-based learning on minority student achievement: Implications for school redesign. *NCPEA Education Leadership Review of Doctoral Research, 2*(2), 50–66.

De La Paz, S., & Hernández-Ramos, P. (2013). Technology-enhanced project-based learning: Effects on historical thinking. *Journal of Special Education Technology, 28*(4), 1–14.

Efstratia, D. (2014). Experiential education through project based learning. *Procedia Social and Behavioral Sciences, 152,* 1256–1260.

Evans, C. M. (2019, December 20). *Student outcomes from high-quality project-based learning: A case study for PBLWorks.* Dover, NH: National Center for the Improvement of Educational Assessment. Accessed at www.pblworks.org/sites/default/files/2020-01/PBLWorks%20HQPBL%20Teacher%20Case%20Study%20Report_FINAL.pdf on April 25, 2024.

Forster, A. G., Bol, T., & van de Werfhorst, H. G. (2016). Vocational education and employment over the life cycle. *Sociological Science, 3,* 473–494.

Fullan, M., & Scott, G. (2014, July). *New pedagogies for deep learning whitepaper: Education PLUS.* Seattle, WA: Collaborative Impact SPC. Accessed at www.michaelfullan.ca/wp-content/uploads/2014/09/Education-Plus-A-Whitepaper-July-2014-1.pdf on September 6, 2024.

Gaertner, D. (2021, November 10). *Increase student ownership with a student-facing project map.* Accessed at https://hthunboxed.org/increase-student-ownership-with-a-student-facing-project-map on April 25, 2024.

Gallagher, S. A. (2015). The role of problem-based learning in developing creative expertise. *Asia Pacific Education Review, 16*(2), 225–235. https://doi.org/10.1007/s12564-015-9367-8

Hutchison, D. (2015, September). *Project-based learning: Drawing on best practices in project management.* Ontario, Canada: Ministry of Education. Accessed at https://drive.google.com/file/d/1V4uu2ODCf0e64kt1_1F8j8_KDaXMqo_N/view on September 6, 2024.

Kwietniewski, K. (2017). *Literature review of project-based learning* [Master's thesis, Buffalo State College]. Buffalo State Digital Commons. https://digitalcommons.buffalostate.edu/careereducation_theses/1.

Larmer, J., & Mergendoller, J. R. (2010). Seven essentials for project-based learning. *Educational Leadership, 68*(1), 34–37.

Lynch, A., (2022). *Project based learning for chronically absent students* [Master's thesis, Hamline University]. School of Education and Leadership Student Capstone Projects. https://digitalcommons.hamline.edu/hse_cp/884.

Mehta, J., & Fine, S. (2019). *In search of deeper learning: The quest to remake the American high school.* Cambridge, MA: Harvard University Press.

Muhammad, A. (2018). *Transforming school culture: How to overcome staff division.* Bloomington, IN: Solution Tree Press.

Murphy, L., Eduljee, N. B., & Croteau, K. (2021). *Teacher-centered versus student-centered teaching: Preferences and differences across academic majors.* Accessed at https://files.eric.ed.gov/fulltext/EJ1304657.pdf on November 25, 2024.

Nachshon, O., & Horowitz-Kraus, T. (2019). Cognitive and emotional challenges in children with reading difficulties. *Acta Paediatrica, 108*(6), 1110–1114.

Pink, D. (2009, July). *The puzzle of motivation* [Video file]. TED Conferences. Accessed at www.ted.com/talks/dan_pink_on_motivation on April 25, 2024.

PowerSchool. (2021, June 14). *Project-based learning: Benefits, examples, and resources* [Blog post]. Accessed at www.powerschool.com/blog/project-based-learning-benefits-examples-and-resources on April 25, 2024.

Prensky, M. (2014). The world needs a new curriculum: It's time to lose the "proxies," and go beyond "21st century skills"—and get all students in the world to the real core of education. *Educational Technology, 54*(4), 3–15.

Roeser, R. W., Eccles, J. S., & Sameroff, A. J. (2000). School as a context of early adolescents' academic and social-emotional development: A summary of research findings. *The Elementary School Journal, 100*(5), 443–471. http://dx.doi.org/10.1086/499650

Ruiz-Rosa, I., Gutiérrez-Taño, D., & García-Rodríguez, F. J. (2021). Project-based learning as a tool to foster entrepreneurial competences. *Cultura y Educación, 33*(2), 316–344. https://doi.org/10.1080/11356405.2021.1904657

Ruth, C., & Ramadas, V. (2019). The "Africanized" competency-based curriculum: The twenty-first century strides. *Shanlax International Journal of Education, 7*(4), 46–51.

Ryerse, M., & Liebtag, E. (2018, August 29). *Project-based learning and the performing arts: A match made in heaven.* Accessed at www.gettingsmart.com/2018/08/29/project-based-learning-and-the-performing-arts-a-match-made-in-heaven on September 6, 2024.

Stanton, M. T., Guerin, S., & Barrett, T. (2017). The transfer of problem-based learning skills to clinical practice. *Interdisciplinary Journal of Problem-Based Learning, 11*(2).

Thomas, J. W. (2000, March). *A review of research on project-based learning*. San Rafael, CA: The Autodesk Foundation. Accessed at www.bobpearlman.org/BestPractices/PBL_Research.pdf on September 6, 2024.

Tyas, N. K., & Fitriani, N. (2021). Enhancing students speaking skills by making video Youtube tutorial as project based learning. *IDEAS: Journal on English Language Teaching and Learning, Linguistics and Literature*, *9*(2), 233–243.

Ummah, S. K., In'am, A., & Azmi, R. D. (2019). Creating manipulatives: Improving students' creativity through project-based learning. *Journal on Mathematics Education*, *10*(1), 93–102.

UNESCO International Bureau of Education. (2017). The why, what and how of competency-based curriculum reforms: The Kenyan experience. *Current and Critical Issues in Curriculum, Learning, and Assessment*, *11*. https://unesdoc.unesco.org/ark:/48223/pf0000250431

Verhaest, D., Lavrijsen, J., Trier, W. V., Nicaise, I., & Omey, E. (2018). General education, vocational education and skill mismatches: Short-run versus long-run effects. *Oxford Economics Papers*, *70*(4), 974–993.

Wang, S. (2022). Critical thinking development through project-based learning. *Journal of Language Teaching and Research*, *13*(5), 1007–1013. https://doi.org/10.17507/jltr.1305.13

World Economic Forum, (2020).

Zhang, L., & Ma, Y. (2023). A study of the impact of project-based learning on student learning effects: a meta-analysis study. *Frontiers in Psychology*, *14*, Article 1202728.

Cory Radisch is the statewide continuous improvement specialist for the New Jersey Department of Education in the Office of Comprehensive Support, working with schools identified for support under the Every Student Succeeds Act.

Throughout his career, Radisch has implemented and developed PLCs at Work, working diligently to transform school culture. In addition to working in schools in New Jersey, Radisch has given presentations and led workshops across the United States on a variety of topics. His main areas of focus are PLCs, positive behavior support in schools, and transforming school culture. He partnered with a school in Honduras for two consecutive summers and is cohost of The Status GROW Podcast. One of the crowning moments of his career is appearing alongside the late Richard DuFour in the endorsements on the back cover of the book *Starting a Movement.*

To learn more about Cory Radisch, visit cradisch.blogspot.com; @moh_consult on X; and Merchant of Hope Consulting on LinkedIn.

To book Cory Radisch for professional development, contact pd@SolutionTree.com.

CHAPTER 4

Making the Shift From Classroom Management to Classroom Leadership

By Cory Radisch

At the beginning of my teaching journey, when students questioned my decisions or directives by asking "Why?" my automatic response was, "Because I said so!" It never occurred to me in my early teaching experience to consider the genuine curiosity behind their questions. I was firmly entrenched in the belief that teaching the way I had been taught was the only correct approach. I perceived any student inquiry as a challenge to my authority, and I responded with phrases reminiscent of those directed at me during my own schooling, such as *Because I am the adult* or *I've paid my dues, now it's your turn*. I was blinded by a sense of unquestionable authority, bolstered by the shiny diploma adorning my wall. I failed to recognize the absurdity of expecting elementary students to appreciate my academic achievements. I erroneously believed that my students should unquestioningly obey me simply because I had endured the rigors of undergraduate studies. My fundamental error lay in assuming that every student should instinctively know how to behave according to my personal ideal of appropriate behavior upon entering the school.

Looking back on this phase of my career, I realize that I was veering toward a Fundamentalist mindset—one of the four educator archetypes education consultant Anthony Muhammad (2018) describes in *Transforming School Culture*. Muhammad (2018) defines the Fundamentalist as an "educator who believes that there is one pure and undisputable way to practice: the traditional model of schooling" (p. 77). In my professional development work with educators, I often refer to the traditional classroom management approach as the *firefighter technique*. This analogy likens the teacher to a firefighter who remains calm until a fire or emergency arises, at which point they spring into action to address the situation. Similarly, many classrooms operate in a reactive manner, with the teacher remaining calm until a disruptive incident occurs, and their response determines whether they successfully resolve the issue or inadvertently escalate it.

In the early stages of my career, I failed to recognize how my response as an adult could contribute to escalating minor issues into major disruptions. My mindset was rooted in the belief that, as the adult authority figure, my instructions should be followed without question. For instance, when faced with a disruptive student in elementary school, my attempts to defuse the situation often backfired. Instead of employing proactive strategies, I reacted impulsively, asking the student, "Is there something wrong with you? Cut it out now!" When met with defiance, I responded with escalating anger, demanding, "I told you to be quiet! Do you understand?" This confrontation not only disrupted the learning environment but also damaged the student-teacher relationship.

Reflecting on these experiences, I now realize that my reactive approach only fueled the conflict further. I took student misbehavior personally and failed to recognize the underlying factors contributing to their behavior. I did not understand that excessive control leads to constant power struggles. I was practicing the accepted traditional approach to handling these types of issues. In retrospect, the school and district assumed teachers had all the tools to meet the goal of reducing discipline issues.

My mistake began with the absence of proactive routines in my classroom. Prior to the experience, I had a lesson that involved group work. My antiquated method of creating groups was to count the number of students and divide that number by the number of groups. I wasted more instructional time by not planning out my groups. One of the biggest complaints I hear from teachers is not having enough time to get through the lesson, the unit, or the curriculum. The proactive routines I share in this chapter will increase instructional time in the classroom, which increases the time for learning.

Establishing a positive classroom experience hinges on distinguishing between rules and expectations. Too often, teachers kick off the year by laying down the law, accompanied by a rules contract requiring parental signatures, often graded as the initial homework assignment. While this traditional method outlines what not to do and its consequences, it fails to engage students proactively. Instead, shifting the paradigm involves setting and teaching expectations and fostering a proactive and respectful classroom atmosphere.

In my presentations across the United States, I've found that students typically recite standard rules like "don't push, run, fight, cheat, or steal" when asked about school or classroom rules. Surprisingly, they offer similar responses when asked about respectful behaviors expected by teachers. This underscores the need to teach behavior as a practiced skill.

Teachers often have concerns about parental involvement when it comes to teaching student behavior. These are valid, but students require ongoing guidance. While most students meet expectations, proactive routines are crucial to prevent disruptions during lessons. Implementing universal classroom expectations, as depicted in the pyramid in figure 4.1 (Center on Positive Behavior Support, n.d.), establishes a foundation for consistent, proactive support and negative behavior prevention at the Tier 1 level.

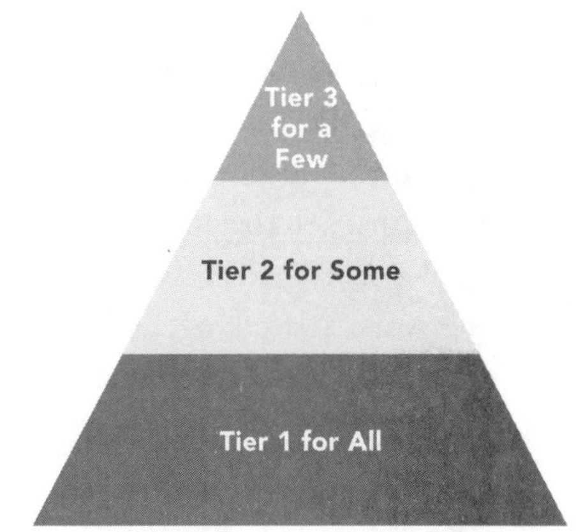

Source: Center on Positive Behavior Support, 2024.

Figure 4.1: The positive behavioral interventions and supports triangle.

As with the response to intervention (RTI) framework, Tier 1 is where mechanisms and systems that promote successful and respectful behavior are put into place for all students. Tier 2 employs strategies for when students do not meet the prosocial and positive expectations that diffuse situations that may escalate into conduct resulting in disciplinary referrals. Tier 3 is dedicated to supporting students who possess more serious behavioral issues. We will discuss strategies for Tier 2 support later in the chapter.

To achieve prevention of negative behavior, educators must consistently communicate expectations during activities and praise students for meeting them, maintaining a positive-to-negative comment ratio of at least 4:1. In the middle school where I was principal, we saw a tremendous decline in discipline referrals after establishing proactive routines and creating protocols for recognizing students who are meeting expectations. One teacher stated that she realized her methods were more combative than connective, but it was the only way she knew before understanding the tenets of positive behavioral interventions and supports and the 4:1 ratio. It's essential to address any concerns about perceived loss of authority; teaching is about fostering hope and opportunity through knowledge, not about exerting control. If the idea of relinquishing authority troubles an educator, teaching might not be the right profession for them.

Implementing Schoolwide Positive Expectations

Reframing classroom rules into positive expectations without using words like *don't* or *no* often poses a challenge. Even new educators struggle with this task because many teachers tend to teach the way they were taught. Let's examine how we can shift from traditional classroom management to classroom leadership using schoolwide positive expectations. You can check the resources for what that looks like. However, if your school has not adopted a positive behavioral interventions and supports framework or something similar, individual teachers, departments, or grade-level teams can certainly implement one on their own. The difficulty lies in crafting positive expectations for every instruction aspect. To begin, consider the behaviors you expect for various activities, such as arrival, dismissal, lining up, submitting homework, group work, partner work, test taking, and free time. Generate a list of what those behaviors look and sound like. Remember, avoid words like *don't*, *can't*, and *no*.

In my experience, teaching others to establish these protocols begins with abstract concepts. For instance, in my presentations, we begin with what I refer to as the three Rs: (1) respectful, (2) responsible, and (3) ready to learn. However, you're welcome to create your own expectations that align with broader schoolwide guidelines. Before delving deeper, let's examine one example using the traditional approach (figure 4.2). Figure 4.3 demonstrates how to transform this approach into a positive one utilizing the three Rs.

Figure 4.2: Classroom management using a traditional approach.

You can either hope for these behaviors to occur daily, or you can actively teach, observe, and acknowledge them using verbal boundaries with students. For instance, as students enter the room, you might greet them and say, "Let's remember the three Rs for arriving to class; we will begin in four minutes." This approach sets a more positive tone than

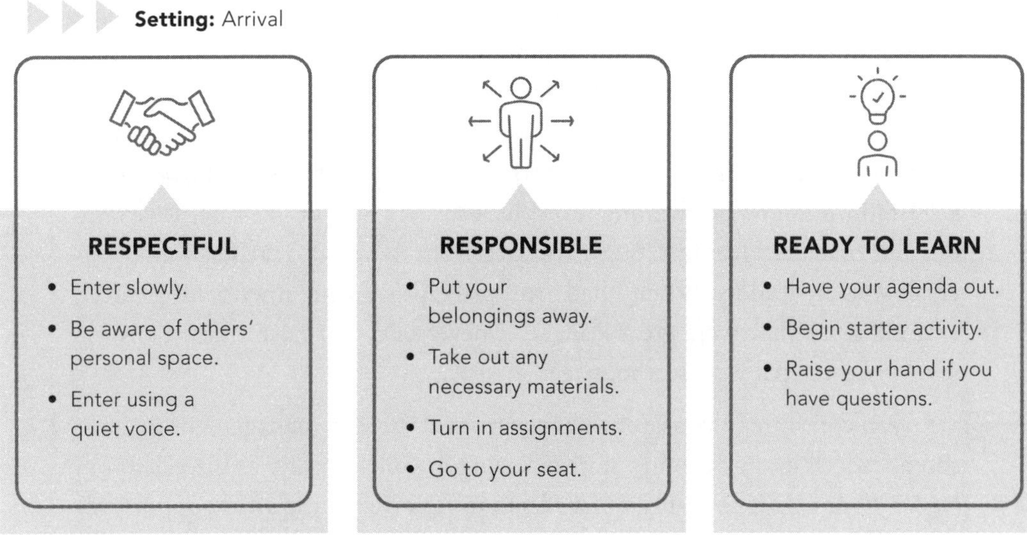

Figure 4.3: Three Rs for a positive approach.

shouting as students enter, "OK, get into class, take your seats, no talking, and begin the starter activity." The former transforms the classroom atmosphere and offers students a prompt for success. In addition, stating instruction will begin in four minutes provides a time boundary. Even better is to have a timer projected on the screen providing the time boundary for when you, as the teacher, will address the class with the day's learning intention. In addition, as students enter, it is crucial to acknowledge them for meeting these expectations. For example, you could say, "I appreciate how Jose, Tom, and Eleana are putting away their belongings and preparing for the lesson." Students thrive on recognition, and if they aren't receiving positive acknowledgment, they may seek negative attention instead. Before we return to universal expectations, I want to stress that the 4:1 positive comment to negative or constructive comments approach—for every negative or constructive comment, four positives are offered—is not confined to education.

For example, psychologist and professor John Gottman's (n.d.) analysis of wedded couples' likelihood of getting divorced or remaining married states the biggest determinant is the ratio of positive to negative comments the partners say to each other. In his research, the ratio was 0.77 to 1 for those who ended up divorced—something like three positive comments for every four negative ones. Furthermore, researchers Marcial Losada and Emily Heaphy (2004) researched the ratio of praise to criticism in sixty business teams in one large company. Teams were identified as high-performing, average, and low-performing based on financial performance, customer satisfaction, and assessments by individual team members. The results were staggering in favor of those leaders who met or exceeded the 4:1 ratio. In their study, high-performing teams have leaders who utilize a 5:1 ratio. Average-performing teams have leaders who utilize a 2:1 ratio, and low-performing teams have leaders who utilize a negative ratio of 1:3 (Losada & Heaphy, 2004). Students want to be led. Teachers want principals who are leaders. When I had great principals during my teaching career, I would say, "They were great leaders." I never said, nor have I heard anyone say, "My principal is a great manager."

As you continue to consider a change from classroom management to classroom leadership, I ask you to start believing in your capacity as the classroom leader. Your role is to lead your students to new heights, provide opportunities, and be merchants of hope.

Recall the firefighter technique I mentioned previously—we typically wait until a problem arises and then respond with punitive measures. With the firefighter technique, our interventions aim for immediate relief in moments of distress by eliminating the issue at hand and assigning responsibility for change to the student or others, such as an administrator. Consider, instead, what I call the Smokey the Bear technique. By adopting universal expectations and adhering to a 4:1 ratio, we adopt a proactive stance akin to that of Smokey the Bear, shifting our focus from reaction to prevention.

Verbal Boundaries

Now, let's delve deeper into the concept of universal expectations, the bottom of the pyramid, and how employing clear verbal boundaries sets students up for success, acting as a strategy to deter misbehavior. Reflecting on my experiences transitioning from classroom management to classroom leadership, let's revisit my earlier approach to group work and my mistakes. Previously, I would hastily form groups based on the number of students present, which wasted instructional time and led to ineffective communication. My instructions often boiled down to a threat: Follow the assignment or risk being removed from the group. This approach conveyed a focus on anticipating misbehavior rather than fostering a conducive learning environment. Effective engagement in collaborative group work begins with strategic planning of groups prior to the lesson. Let's outline the components of group work in a classroom using established proactive routines that have been practiced beforehand.

1. Establish groups prior to the lesson.
2. State clear directions for the learning intention with an opportunity for students to ask clarifying questions.
3. Review previously established expectations (adult meetings call these *norms*) for group work.
4. Provide students with the allotted time and circulate to formatively assess students.
5. Use a previously established routine for students and groups seeking assistance.
6. Provide a countdown alerting students to how much time is left in the activity as you circulate the room. Project a timer on the board and use a preestablished signal for students to return to their seats.

Let's dissect each of these components and the language used to create proactive expectations that provide students with opportunities for success rather than assuming students will meet expectations and then being reactive when they do not.

Establish Groups Prior to the Lesson

Establish groups prior to the lesson to prevent potential embarrassment to students. Creating groups on the spot can lead to situations where students are publicly singled out and excluded, which can be demoralizing. For example, saying something like, "OK, you four are a group, no wait, you two can't work together, so you (pointing at one student) stand over there for a second," can ostracize the student singled out and make them feel isolated. While this may seem trivial, it's important to avoid such situations to maintain a positive and inclusive classroom environment. Teachers should use classroom data beforehand to form groups when activities involve classroom performance and students rotating to address each other's needs. In my experience, displaying the daily agenda on the board to inform students about group work and list groups was beneficial. In my classroom, I fostered a culture of inclusion and appreciation, where students were reminded that they were expected to be open-minded and prepared to collaborate effectively even if they weren't particularly fond of the classmates in their group.

State Clear Directions

During the early stages of my teaching career, I often made the mistake of hastily sending students off to work in groups without providing clear and concise directions, including the objective and expected outcomes. I would fret about time constraints and assume students understood what to do, especially as the school year progressed. However, this often led to confusion, with students raising their hands or shouting out questions like, “Hey, Mr. R, what are we supposed to do?” This confusion spread to other groups, derailing the lesson as I had to repeatedly explain the directions. I recall many instances of frustration when lessons ran out of time, forcing us to carry over the activity to the next day.

Consider the following tips when giving directions for group work.

- Ensure the directions are age-appropriate, as sometimes we unintentionally express objectives and directions in a way more suited for adults.
- Clearly articulate the knowledge students will gain from the activity. For instance, say, “After our collaborative work today, you will be able to construct arguments for or against why the main character should engage the company president with their proposal.” This should align with the learning objective displayed on the board, focusing on writing persuasive essays with clearly stated positions or opinions.
- Provide a step-by-step breakdown of what students will do during the group activity. For example, say, “In your pre-assigned groups, you will read the passage provided in each area. Once everyone has finished reading, discuss the questions listed on the handout and collaboratively create a paragraph on the index card in your group’s space, ensuring it aligns with the expectations outlined.”
- Allow time for clarifying questions from students.
- Engage students in a turn-and-talk activity where they share, in their own words, the established learning intention.

It’s important to note that the previous instructions focus solely on what students will do and learn during the collaborative activity. Many teachers may stop here and proceed to group work without addressing or reviewing behavioral expectations. However, the next component is crucial for setting students up for a successful group activity.

Review Previously Established Expectations, Provide Students With the Allotted Time, and Use a Previously Established Signal to Begin Work

This is the not-so-secret sauce for putting students on the correct path for meeting objectives. It doesn't take more than a minute, especially if group work routines have been previously established and practiced. This section describes steps three through five and how they set students up for success prior to starting group work. This is what it would sound like: "Students, we are about to engage in a group activity. Take fifteen seconds to turn and talk with your neighbor and share at least one expectation we have established for group work."

This scenario illustrates the importance of establishing clear verbal boundaries as opposed to assuming understanding. Explicitly informing students that they have fifteen seconds to turn and talk provides a concrete time constraint for the activity. As the fifteen seconds nears its end, I typically announce, "OK, time is winding down." Even if the discussion extends beyond the allocated fifteen seconds, this announcement signals to students that the conversation period is concluding.

The next step is to employ the preestablished signal to regain the class's focus. In my case, I would prompt with, "Students, can I have your attention," and proceed to count down aloud from three to one. This countdown allows students a moment to wrap up their thoughts. To further facilitate success, I might add, "Clap your hands if you heard my countdown from three to one." When those who have refocused clap, it serves as a signal to other students that it's time to redirect their attention.

Subsequently, I might prompt students to share the topics they discussed regarding group expectations. Referring to figure 4.4 (page 66), I would then address any expectations that were not covered and project the expectations for group work onto the screen for clarity.

Before instructing students to leave their seats, it's important to establish a verbal time boundary for the activity. For instance, I might say, "Students, you will have fifteen minutes to complete the activity." I then ask the entire class to echo back the time boundary. This simple act ensures students are aware of the allotted time, which prevents surprise when time is up. Without this clear time boundary, students may be caught off guard or request additional time, claiming they didn't realize how much time had passed. Providing the time boundary along with incremental countdowns helps students remain focused and on task.

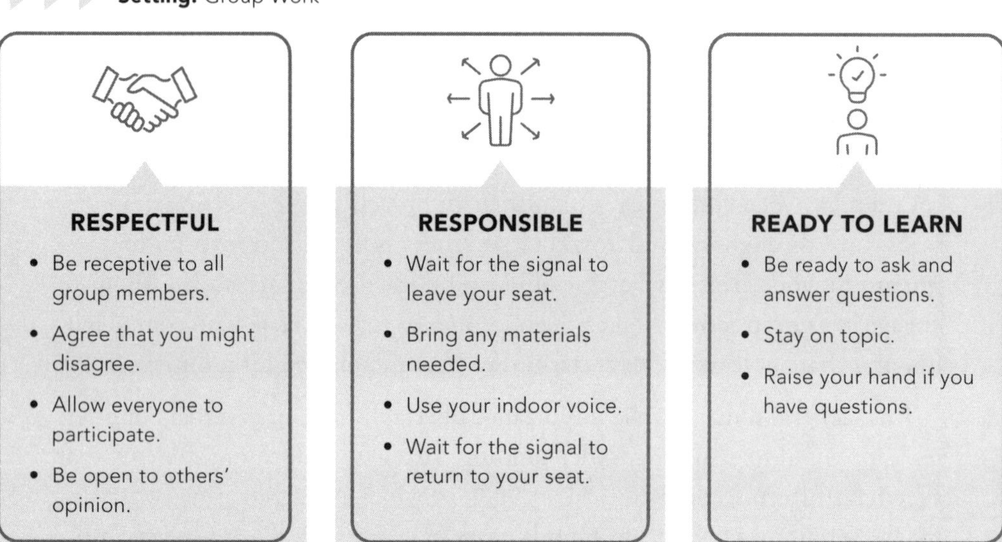

Figure 4.4: Expectations for group work.

Once the time boundary is set, we proceed to use our preestablished signal to initiate group work. In my experience, I promote that students are involved in developing these protocols, empowering them to contribute to the classroom environment. Often, students choose a common signal such as *go*, but I've also encountered creative examples, like a class using a computer sound mimicking the start of a NASCAR race. Remarkably, because these signals are practiced and familiar, they don't result in chaotic movements; instead, students move safely and efficiently to their designated locations.

Utilize Student Work Time for Formative Assessment

The teacher circulates the room providing feedback and assessing learning during the group activity. With a fifteen-minute activity, a teacher should aim to visit each group two to three times, using this opportunity for formative assessment. This may include keeping track of student progress on a roster with simple plus or minus symbols to indicate understanding of the material.

While observing students, it is crucial to recognize groups that meet behavioral expectations. Use specific feedback and avoid general praise like *good job*. Instead, overtly praise expected behaviors, acknowledging individual groups or publicly recognizing them. Specific praise might sound like, "Group two, I appreciate how quickly you assembled and began the task." It's also important to acknowledge specific expectations from figure 4.4, such as, "Gina, I appreciate your respectful disagreement with Tyrone," which reinforces the desired behavior. Professor John Hattie (n.d.), in his research on influences on student achievement, gave high-quality feedback an effect size of 0.78 with a 0.4 effect size equaling one year's growth in one year's time. His research shares that high-quality feedback has the potential for almost two years growth in one year's time.

Addressing groups that stray off-task involves subtle interventions. For instance, if a group becomes chatty or off-topic, I might praise another group nearby for meeting expectations, encouraging the off-task group to refocus. If needed, a gentle prompt like, "Do you feel you're meeting group expectations right now?" helps redirect behavior without admonishment. The goal isn't punishment but behavior change, and this approach is often effective in getting students back on track.

Use a Preestablished Signal for Students Seeking Assistance

One behavior that frustrates teachers is when students consistently get out of their seats to seek assistance with the learning. There are a variety of strategies that allow you to circulate the room to work with individual students or groups and avoid this frustration. My favorite strategy to use is a laminated square with a question mark. Students can raise the square to seek my assistance, and I will go over and assist the student or group if I am free. However, if I am working with another individual student or group, I acknowledge the square and the student then places it in the predetermined space on their desk. This is like the raised-hand feature on a Zoom call.

Another strategy is the parking lot. For this strategy, there is a predetermined place on the whiteboard labeled *parking lot*. Students are free to get out of their seat and write their question in the parking lot. If the class is working individually, the student writes their initials. If the class is working in groups, they write the group number or name. This helps the teacher assist students in order and avoids student frustration when they feel they may have been skipped over for assistance.

Use a Preestablished Signal to End the Activity

As the activity approaches its end, the screen displays the diminishing time and the teacher verbally announces the remaining time. When the timer reaches zero, the teacher employs a preestablished signal to regain the class's focus. As a reminder, I typically use the phrase, "Students, can I have your attention" and count backward from three. Once students have redirected their attention and each group has shared their work, it's time to signal them to return to their seats using our established procedure. That sounds like this: "All right, I appreciate everyone's dedication to learning and the work you've produced. Please gather your materials and listen for the signal to return to your seats." My signal is a simple clap of my hands. I often use this technique in my presentations with adults, and it always amuses me how some individuals scurry back to their seats at the sound of the clap. It's crucial to recognize that humans naturally seek structure (Frey, Störmer, & Willführ, 2011), and when this structure is clearly articulated, most individuals will comply with the expectations.

However, it's important to acknowledge that as students begin returning to their seats after the clap, some may lag. This delay may occur as they finish their thoughts or tasks. In such instances, I address the class by saying, "Raise your hand if you heard me clap." This prompts students who haven't yet returned to their seats to take notice, as they observe others raising their hands. This action serves as an alert that the activity has concluded and it's time to return to their seats. This approach fosters a more tranquil environment compared to loudly announcing the end of the activity and escalating volume when students don't immediately comply.

Strategies for Individual Student Noncompliance

After my transformation to classroom leadership, I was teaching a grade 8 class in which there was a student who was chronically disciplined. We will call him Joe. During one lesson, the students were working individually on a writing assignment while I circulated the room to assist. Joe, who was frustrated by the assignment, shouted out, "This is the worst [expletive] class in the school!" I ignored the statement and kept helping other students. Seeing as he did not get a reaction from me, Joe repeated his statement this time without the expletive. I ignored it again but when he did it a third time, I calmly went to him and employed the fogging strategy (Henry, 2006).

This strategy transfers the struggle to the student's head. Here is what I said: "Joe, thank you for your opinion. That is possible. What do you think we can do to make this class better? Let's talk after class." This strategy did a few things. The first and most important is that it did not include a raised reaction. Second, I transferred the problem back to the student by asking him for solutions. Third, I let him know that what he was doing by shouting out was unacceptable and we would be talking about it later. The situation was already de-escalated when he didn't get the raised reaction he was seeking and learning could continue. Let's explore a few of my other favorite strategies.

Language of Choice

Some students want power or control. The best way to give someone limited control is through choices. The only way to teach students responsibility and accountability is to provide choices and then hold them accountable for those choices. For example, "Joe, you have a choice to return to your seat or you will need to leave the room. I know you will make a great choice." Once you say this, get quiet and disengage from the student. One of the biggest mistakes educators make is hovering over the student. This doesn't allow the student to freely make either the right or wrong choice but sends the message, I have power over you, and I will wait here until you do what is right. If the student makes the right choice and returns to their seat, bravo! If they don't, you will have to follow through and have them removed from the classroom. As the class leader, you must be prepared when the student makes the wrong choice.

"Save It For . . ." Statements

Remember, the goal is to get a change in the behavior before you resort to a consequence. This strategy addresses students' inappropriate behavior but with a different approach. Remember some behavior is not bad, it's just not appropriate in the setting. See the following examples of this strategy.

- "Joe, save the running for physical education. I'm excited to see the work you produce."
- "Joe, save the talking for the group work activity coming up. Don't waste it all now."

We can address unwanted behavior by simply rephrasing our words in a way that demonstrates respect and is likely not to escalate the situation.

"I Will" or "I Notice" Statements

Once again, this strategy acknowledges that the student is not meeting expectations; however, it lets the student know that you are the leader of the classroom. The following are some examples of this.

- "I will call on you when you raise your hand. Thanks for understanding."
- "I notice you are not doing your work. What can I do to help you get back on track?"

Both question statements simultaneously address the issue and offer praise or empower the student to make a decision. In the first statement, the teacher has provided another strategy called preemptive thanks (Spencer, 2006). In this strategy, the teacher thanks the student prior to them complying to raise their hand. Teachers can use this strategy with the whole class or individual students. To use this with the whole class, you may say something like, "Students, I need to thank you before we even get started. I know you are going to meet expectations today, and I'm going to get so excited over the work you produce I might forget to say thank you." I like to use this strategy with an individual student, especially if we had a difficult time the day before. For example, I may greet the student prior to entering the room and say, "Joe, I want to thank you because I have a feeling today is going to be a much better day than yesterday. I am glad we are starting fresh. Have a great class." In the second statement, the teacher is alerting the student they were not on task, but instead of escalating with different language, the teacher offers assistance. With either statement, and as stated in the section on language of choice, don't hover over the student. Instead, disengage and give the student room to hopefully make the right choice.

Asking the Right Questions

One of the biggest mistakes we can make with students that often escalates a situation is asking them the wrong questions when addressing misbehavior. I found myself making this mistake frequently during the initial stages of my teaching journey, leading to disruptive events in the classroom that hindered learning for all.

Often, I would ask questions expecting a specific answer, and I perceived it as disrespectful if the student didn't provide that answer and resorted to writing a discipline referral. For example, have you ever asked a student if they think you look stupid? There are only two possible answers to that question: yes or no. However, we often fail to prepare ourselves for the possibility that the student might answer yes, leading to frustration and anger when they do. Another example is asking, "How many times do I have to tell you . . . ?" By phrasing questions like this, we unintentionally give students the freedom to answer however they see fit. I've had students respond to this question with, "I think you have to tell me thirty-two more times," which only fueled my frustration and initiated unnecessary back-and-forth exchanges that could have been avoided.

Instead, consider using more effective questioning techniques. For instance, "Joe, are you aware of the directions for this activity? Yes or no?" If Joe answers yes, respond with encouragement, saying, "Great, I look forward to seeing you in action." If Joe replies no, offer support by saying, "I apologize if I didn't explain the directions clearly enough. Let me go over them again to ensure your success."

Similarly, with another student named Jacey, you might ask, "Jacey, are we working on page forty-six, questions one through five? Yes or no?" If Jacey says yes, you can challenge her by saying, "Well, it seems we have different definitions of working. Let's see you put in a better effort." If she says no, offer assistance by saying, "Actually, the other students are working on page forty-six. Is there anything I can do to help you succeed?"

It's crucial to disengage and give the student space to make their own choices after presenting these options. Avoid immediately jumping back into disciplinary action. Disengaging sends a message that you trust and empower students to make the right decisions, while hovering implies that you'll make the choice for them. Remember, it's better to be proactive in addressing misbehavior than to react impulsively.

Positive Behavioral Interventions and Supports and School Culture

Both Muhammad's (2018) work on school culture and positive behavioral interventions and supports aim to create supportive, effective learning environments, though they approach this goal from slightly different angles. At their core, both frameworks are united by a common purpose: improving student outcomes by fostering a positive and proactive school culture.

Positive behavioral interventions and supports are grounded in prevention and proactive intervention. It operates with the understanding that creating a structured environment—one that encourages and rewards positive behaviors—will reduce the need for reactive discipline. Positive behavioral interventions and supports involve defining clear behavioral expectations, teaching these behaviors explicitly, and providing consistent reinforcement for positive behavior while addressing challenging behavior with targeted support strategies. The approach is data-driven, focusing on setting clear expectations, monitoring progress, and making necessary adjustments to improve school climate.

Muhammad (2018) focuses on changing the fundamental attitudes and beliefs within a school to create a more positive, collaborative environment. He emphasizes the importance of addressing and shifting the school's cultural norms and beliefs to overcome barriers to student success. His framework involves engaging staff in reflective practices, fostering a sense of shared responsibility, and building a culture where high expectations are the norm.

Muhammad (2018) and positive behavioral interventions and supports share a fundamental commitment to creating supportive, effective learning environments. By focusing on clear expectations, proactive strategies, collaboration, data-driven practices, and professional development, both frameworks work in concert to improve school culture and enhance student success. Their alignment reflects a comprehensive approach to educational improvement, where cultural transformation and behavioral support can reinforce each other to foster a thriving school environment.

Conclusion

Before I shifted into a classroom leadership role, I grappled with students whom I perceived as purposefully disrupting my lessons. There were instances when I had to enlist the support of my vice-principal to regain control of the class. This challenge stemmed from two primary factors: (1) I had not cultivated strong connections with each student, and (2) I took student misbehavior personally instead of addressing it professionally. I often relied solely on punitive measures rather than approaching the behavior with a focus on teaching, practice, and positive reinforcement.

I've noticed that schools where teachers have altered their approaches tend to see a decrease in discipline referrals, particularly from the classroom. As educators, we have the choice to lead our classrooms by enforcing rules, enabling leniency, or empowering students. For me, genuine progress in my teaching journey occurred when I embraced an empowering approach. After my transformation, I found myself feeling less fatigued at the end of each day because I prioritized uplifting and motivating my students.

Please understand that it takes time to transform your practices. You need to plan and practice for the shift. It won't happen overnight. However, once you get the hang of it, I can assure you that you will successfully create more time for learning and decrease the time spent on correcting behaviors. These strategies, when practiced in a classroom, will help create a community of learners using respect, routine, and hope. When practiced schoolwide, these strategies can assist in transforming your school's culture.

References and Resources

Casas, J. (2017). *Culturize: Every student, every day, whatever it takes.* San Diego, CA: Dave Burgess Consulting.

Center on Positive Behavior Support. (2024). *What is PBIS?* Accessed at www.pbis.org/pbis/what-is-pbis on September 11, 2024.

Eskreis-Winkler, L., & Fishback, A. (2020). When praise—versus criticism—motivates goal pursuit. In E. Brummelman (Ed.), *Psychological Perspectives on Praise* (pp. 47–54). London: Routledge.

Frey, U. J., Störmer, C., & Willführ, K. P. (2011). *Essential building blocks of human nature.* Berlin, Germany: Springer.

Gottman, J. (n.d.). *Marriage and couples.* Accessed at www.gottman.com/about/research/couples on April 25, 2024.

Hattie, J. (n.d.). *Hattie ranking: 252 influences and effect sizes related to student achievement.* Accessed at https://visible-learning.org/hattie-ranking-influences-effect-sizes-learning-achievement on April 25, 2024.

Henry, S. (2006). *Practical strategies for working successfully with difficult, noncompliant students (grades 6–12).* Bellevue, WA: Bureau of Education and Research.

Losada, M., & Heaphy, E. (2004). The role of positivity and connectivity in the performance of business teams: A nonlinear dynamics model. *American Behavioral Scientist, 47*(6), 740–765. https://doi.org/10.1177/0002764203260208

Mathews, I. (2021, March 8). *Praise versus criticism: What is the ideal ratio?* Accessed at https://5on4.group/what-is-the-ideal-mix-of-praise-versus-criticism on April 25, 2024.

Muhammad, A. (2018). *Transforming school culture: How to overcome staff division.* Bloomington, IN: Solution Tree Press.

Muhammad, A., & Cruz, L. F. (2019) *Time for change: 4 essential skills for transformational school and district leaders.* Bloomington, IN: Solution Tree Press.

Spencer, H. (2006). *Practical strategies for working with difficult, noncompliant students (grades 6–12).* Bellevue, WA: Bureau of Education and Research.

Zenger, J., & Folkman, J. (2013, March 15). *The ideal praise-to-criticism ratio.* Accessed at https://hbr.org/2013/03/the-ideal-praise-to-criticism on October 6, 2023.

Kathy Vergara, EdD, is an experienced educator dedicated to improving educational outcomes for multilingual learners and their families. She serves as the director of the multilingual department in a large Southeast Texas public school district, focusing on designing and implementing curricula for bilingual, dual-language, and multilingual programs in grades preK–12.

Dr. Vergara has extensive experience designing, implementing, and delivering equitable curricula with a focus on biliteracy. She has served at the state level on the Dual Language Guidance Committee and the Communities of Practice committee, concentrating on biliteracy and dual language education. In 2021, Dr. Vergara was recognized by the Texas Education Agency's English Learner Program for providing equitable opportunities through the strategic rollout of biliteracy curricula and pedagogy across eighteen campuses. Additionally, in 2023, she was honored by the Texas Association for Bilingual Education as a Public Education Honoree for her commitment to bilingual education and to linguistically and culturally diverse students in Texas.

Dr. Vergara also serves on the executive board of the Houston Area Association for Bilingual Education. She has presented as an associate at the Solution Tree *Soluciones* conference, focusing on educational successes for Latinx students using research-based and equitable practices. Dr. Vergara has been a district instructional officer, language specialist, and bilingual/dual language teacher at a Model PLC at Work campus. She participated in a national fellowship focused on closing educational gaps for Latinx students and the Harvard University Closing the Gap program. Passionate about shifting mindsets to better support historically underserved students, Dr. Vergara advocates for equitable opportunities in education.

She earned her undergraduate degree in Spanish and business management from the University of Houston, a master's degree in educational psychology with an emphasis on bilingual and dual-language education from Texas A&M, and a second master's degree in educational leadership for culturally and linguistically diverse students. She holds a doctorate in ethical leadership from the University of St. Thomas in Houston.

To learn more about Kathy Vergara and her work, visit @Kathy_Vergara2 on X.

To schedule Kathy Vergara for professional development, contact pd@SolutionTree.com.

CHAPTER 5

Navigating Bias and Building Respect and Trust

By Kathy Vergara

Growing up as a first-generation Latina student in the United States, my journey through the educational system was marked by triumphs and challenges. Language and culture were integral to my navigation through academia, both positively and negatively shaping my experiences. While I excelled when inspired by passionate teachers and engaging subjects, the pervasive sense of being an outsider often overshadowed my potential.

My experience as a third grader illustrated this feeling of being an outsider as I was pulled for English language instruction, often referred to as English as a second language (ESL) instruction, for thirty minutes a few times a week, which I found embarrassing and isolating even at age eight. English was taught in isolation with outdated magnetic people on the whiteboard that reviewed words like family, mom, and dad. I remember thinking, *I am not in kindergarten; why am I here?* The situation was heightened when my classmates questioned why I was pulled out by an English language instruction teacher during our time for group work. Eight-year-old me quickly learned the pickup time, and I conveniently went to the restroom or volunteered to take anything to the office a few minutes before the English language instruction teacher showed up.

This started a love-hate, toxic relationship with the schooling system. I had a genuine love for learning, especially when the subject was engaging and the teacher was inspiring; unfortunately, those experiences were exceptions rather than the norm. Most of the time I felt like an outsider, unable to compete with my peers, and many of my teachers inadvertently reinforced this message. My cumulative folder was adorned with labels, such as *limited English proficiency*, *at risk*, *low socioeconomic status*, *mild behavior problem*, *talks a lot*, and *not engaged*, along with the unwritten descriptions of immigrant and whose mother had her in high school. When I compared myself to the other students who were frequently celebrated at the classroom and school level, they hardly resembled me—they were born in the United States and spoke English fluently. They never had to sit through parent-teacher conferences translating what the teacher was conveying, nor did they find themselves making calls to the electric company on behalf of their grandparents due to language barriers. No, those kids were like the ones portrayed in my favorite sitcoms, with a two-parent household and cars to match. They did not have to explain the intricacies of a slumber party to their parents or justify spending the night at a friend's house.

Much of my time in grades K–8 was spent striving to find acceptance among the right friends, which I eventually did while attempting to evade the spotlight of teachers who often made me feel inferior. This dichotomy fueled my determination to create inclusive and supportive learning environments as an educator, particularly for historically marginalized students like Latinx multilingual learners. As I grew older, I shed the fear of rejection by my teachers and adopted a more confrontational demeanor, perceiving it as an act of defiance. However, this approach proved counterproductive, leading to the addition of more preconceived ideas about me in the classroom.

My trajectory shifted during my sophomore year of high school when my teacher, Ms. Semi, recommended me for the honors class during course selection. Initially, I assumed it was a mistake; I often received side-eye for talking out of turn and distracting others. Ms. Semi assured me it wasn't an error and attributed my behavior to needing more of a challenge. She saw potential in me that I hadn't recognized in myself. Her belief in my abilities was a turning point; it transformed my mindset and propelled me to excel. The following year, I worked harder than ever in the honors class, driven to prove I was good enough to myself and my teachers. I loved reading, analyzing, and discussing *The Great Gatsby*, *The Awakening*, and *The Scarlet Letter*. I was thrilled and surprised to realize that I had meaningful contributions to add to the conversation.

This pivotal moment defined my academic journey and inspired my educational career path, demonstrating how a teacher's belief can genuinely change lives. Despite the labels and perceptions, Ms. Semi's unwavering belief in me instilled the conviction that all students can learn and flourish given the right environment and support. I now realize that Ms. Semi exemplified what education consultant and author Anthony Muhammad (2018) describes as a Believer—a teacher who sees beyond the surface and believes all students can learn at high levels and are not defined by labels and shallow perceptions. Ms. Semi shifted the trajectory of my life by believing in me, thus transforming my mindset to believe in myself. Despite encountering numerous teachers who failed to see my potential, it only took one to recognize the version of me that had yet to develop fully.

As a result of my experience with Ms. Semi, I entered the teaching field with an unwavering belief in all students' potential. I understood the efficacy of bilingual education when implemented correctly. Driven by a hunger for knowledge and a desire to make a difference, I embraced my students' unique needs, adapting my approach as necessary. Mirroring my experience with Ms. Semi, I believed in myself and my students, leading to remarkable outcomes. My students' success—measured through various metrics, such as state achievement tests, engagement, and behavior—became my instructional norm. Therefore, I proudly identify as a Believer, as illustrated in Muhammad's (2018) work on positive school culture, demonstrating the power of such teachers in education and their profound impact on students' lives.

Navigating biases and my own feelings of otherness throughout my K–12 journey empowered me to take control of my experiences instead of remaining a bystander. This process also helped me develop trust in the schooling system, leveraging it to foster personal growth. Acknowledging my privilege, I realized the importance of using it to open doors for others, ensuring future students would not face the same obstacles.

Navigating Bias

Early in my career as a bilingual teacher in a large suburban district, I approached my team lead to inform her about a new student, Natalie, who was enrolled in her class. During the open house, her parents mentioned that Natalie had participated in the bilingual program at her previous school, which I confirmed by checking her cumulative folder. I intended to make roster changes to ensure Natalie continued receiving bilingual services. The conversation unfolded as follows with my grade-level team lead.

> ***Me:*** Hi, Ms. Parker. I noticed Natalie was on your roster, but she comes from a bilingual program—I believe she should be placed in my class.
>
> ***Ms. Parker [Prepping for the next class and passing out papers without looking up]:*** What? I don't think so. That must be a mistake. She is actually really smart.

I couldn't believe what I was hearing. Countless thoughts raced through my mind, leaving me dumbfounded. Did my grade-level lead think my students weren't intelligent? Did she think I wasn't smart enough as a second-language learner? Her articulation of this deficit perception of my students left me at a loss. How could I share my students during our intervention block if she held such a low opinion of them?

I now understand that she displayed what professor of educational psychology Richard R. Valencia (1997) describes as a deficit mindset toward students in a bilingual program and those learning English as a second language. This mindset, referred to as *educability*, suggests that students from historically marginalized backgrounds need to be remediated through intervention to meet what is perceived as the norm (Valencia, 1997). Traditionally, for students learning English as a second language, this mindset results in not exposing students to grade-level standards to prioritize English development. This mirrors my own experience of being pulled out for English language instruction while my classmates engaged in collaborative activities. In hindsight, this was counterproductive since collaborative activities promote more authentic language production. Ms. Parker succumbed to the deficit mindset that educational leadership author and presenter Kenneth C. Williams (2022) describes in his book *Ruthless Equity: Disrupt the Status Quo and Ensure Learning for All Students* as complacency with the status quo. Like many other well-intentioned educators, she assumed that bilingual education was a remedial class designed solely to teach students English and prepare them for a mainstream setting.

After our brief interaction, I stood at Ms. Parker's doorstep feeling dumbfounded for what felt like hours as I tried to figure out what to say and how to say it. After all, I was in a professional setting; the situation could escalate very quickly if I lost my cool. However, walking away without saying anything would signal my complacency and perpetuate her bias. Worst of all, I was afraid I would cry in front of her and appear weak or like a victim, and I was determined not to let that happen. Despite wanting to respond in numerous ways, all I could manage at that moment was to stammer, "Being in a bilingual program does not mean you are not smart."

She finally looked up from her paperwork with a surprised expression, as if I had offended her, and said, "Oh no, that's not what I meant. I mean—she is doing so well here; I don't think she needs support. Sorry—in my other district, struggling students were put in bilingual classes; that's been my experience." It took every ounce of strength to hold back my tears, nod, and walk away.

That moment has played on repeat in my mind for years. I envisioned it ending with a powerful comeback that could reshape Ms. Parker's perspective. Instead, I walked away carrying a weight of resentment and a deep distrust toward my teammate's understanding of my students' needs. I shut the door, both literally and figuratively, on that conversation, determined to prove my students' incredible potential. My reaction echoes Muhammad's (2018) insights about Believers in toxic school environments—they retreat to their classrooms, steadfastly supporting their students. Still, the collaborative spirit of the learning community suffers as a result.

I wish I could say my story and experiences are unique and that educators of all kinds did not have similar stories of encountering microaggressions toward multilingual learners. Unfortunately, this everyday experience is just one among many. Thankfully, with time, age, wisdom, and experience, my responses have evolved, yet the sting of each microaggression lingers. Termed *death by a thousand papercuts*, microaggressions are pervasive experiences defined as "acts that can usually be explained away by seemingly unbiased and valid reasons. For the recipient of a microaggression, however, there is always the nagging question of whether it really happened" (Crocker & Major, 1989; Sue et al., 2007; Sue & Spanierman, 2020). I developed distrust because of the numerous papercuts throughout my educational and professional journey. While PLCs emphasize the benefits and power of building and sustaining collaborative teams, achieving this can be easier said than done. How can I trust educators who have been so critical of me and the students who share my background?

Building Respect and Trust

Building trust and respect in educational settings across stakeholders is foundational to creating an inclusive and supportive environment for all students. I have encountered numerous instances of bias and prejudice within educational settings as a bilingual educator. From assumptions about students' capabilities based on their language backgrounds to microaggressions directed toward multilingual learners, the prevalence of bias poses significant challenges to fostering trust and respect among colleagues.

The foundation of trust and respect must be established before incidents of bias occur. According to a literature review on trust in education, trust is a fundamental component for effective communication in any organizational team (Niedlich, Kallfass, Pohle, & Bormann, 2021). For instance, teammates start to understand each other's backgrounds and learn to navigate difficult conversations through the development of norms (Niedlich et al., 2021). Even in a positive culture with boundaries as Muhammad (2018) describes, people can have difficult conversations. Professors Özlem Sensoy and Robin DiAngelo (2014) refer to this work as *creating common guidelines* when navigating volatile discussions and topics of social justice in education.

Norms are an integral part of the PLC process, where members establish the purpose, goals, and behaviors that drive or inhibit the target of working collaboratively to ensure every student succeeds. The execution of norms and how members reset team behaviors when a norm is broken can vary from meeting to meeting. I've seen educators use the word *squirrel* to indicate a deviation in expectations. In another PLC, teams had a picture of the Cheers television show character Norm on a paddle, and someone would raise it whenever the team went off track. These verbal and visual reminders served to reset conversations and behaviors, refocusing the energy back on the purpose and goals.

These attention-getters are effective within meetings, but a true PLC goes beyond a collaborative meeting. A PLC is a mindset, the tone and culture of a school, and how the adults in the system view students and themselves within the school's ecosystem. The challenge lies in addressing norms outside the typical meeting and ensuring continued collaboration beyond the four walls.

SCAN Approach

To ensure effective collaboration, the team must adopt a proactive approach that extends beyond mere norm resets. PLCs are characterized by continuous improvement processes that demand ongoing collaboration and calibration to ensure alignment in mindsets and outcomes. However, have you ever been in a room full of passionate educators? Conflicts are inevitable, but they can ultimately strengthen the team and improve student outcomes. The key lies in navigating these conflicts to foster a culture of trust and collaboration centered on shared beliefs.

This is where the SCAN framework comes into play. SCAN stands for self, commitment, advocacy, and norms—four critical components designed to build and sustain trust within teams. Self involves starting with personal reflection to understand and address one's biases. Commitment requires a dedicated focus on maintaining equitable practices and fostering an inclusive environment. Advocacy encourages team members to leverage their privilege to support and elevate marginalized voices. Finally, norms emphasize establishing and adhering to agreed-on behaviors and practices that respect and celebrate diversity. Remember to SCAN when striving to cultivate a culture of trust within your collaborative teacher teams.

Self

Start with the self. Developing self-awareness through a reflective process is imperative. Everyone brings conscious and unconscious biases to the meeting table and the classroom regardless of their self-identification. This doesn't make anyone a bad person; it makes them human. The key is acknowledging these biases and reflecting on how they can impact students. This topic can be sensitive, and not everyone may be ready or willing to engage in self-reflection and sharing. Everyone's lived experiences are different and influence their comfort level. However, as a profession, we can initiate a process of self-reflection to build self-awareness. This self-reflective process could be incorporated into the closing of a collaborative meeting—everyone takes five minutes to reflect on the discussion and has a safe space to share if desired.

Commitment

Developing self-awareness will lead your team to recalibrate their commitment to the principles of educational equity and what that looks like in action. It is a commitment to understanding that, as individuals, we don't know everything, and everyone has strengths to contribute to the greater good. It is a commitment to continuous improvement, recognizing that we don't have to continue doing things the same way just because we've always done them that way. It is a commitment to being open and eager to learn and understand for the sake of your team and, more importantly, your students.

Advocacy

Part of the SCAN model, through self-reflection and building awareness, is acknowledging the privileges we each bring to the table. This is not meant to pit one person against another, nor is it a tabulation. Recognizing privileges allows educators to leverage them to ally with historically marginalized educators and students, resulting in advocacy. This involves acknowledging and addressing our own biases and actively advocating for policies, practices, and resources that promote equity and inclusion in education. It means speaking up for students whose voices may not be heard, amplifying their stories, and championing their rights to access quality education.

Norms

Establishing norms is pivotal in fostering a culture of trust within a team. However, norms must extend beyond mere politeness to truly foster educational equity. This involves navigating challenging conversations and questioning the status quo that has historically marginalized diverse learners. Throughout the collaborative process of setting norms, it is essential to acknowledge that all decisions and inquiries are made with the students' best interests at heart. The norms should emphasize respecting and celebrating diversity within the team and among the students being served. Teams commit to being reflective, continuously learning, advocating for all students, and engaging in discussions centered on the work. Additionally, effective collaborative teams welcome pushback and view it not as a personal threat but as an opportunity to question ideas rather than people.

Figure 5.1 provides a summary of the SCAN framework.

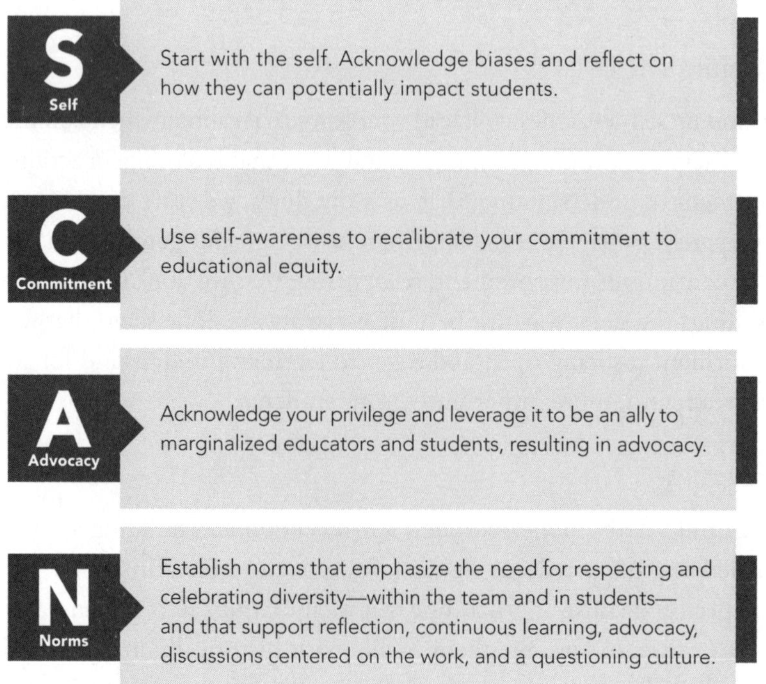

Figure 5.1: SCAN framework.

Conclusion

I was hurt by Ms. Parker's comments because of my lived experiences as an immigrant multilingual learner who navigated the waters of bilingual and English language instruction and constantly felt like I did not belong in the mainstream educational setting. In retrospect, what I did not acknowledge during the encounter with Ms. Parker—through my frustration and pain—was that I had an opportunity. I was a college-educated professional, a teacher speaking with my colleague who had enough information to articulate her uninformed misgivings. I had privileges that many others from historically marginalized communities, including those from my ethnic and linguistic backgrounds, did not have. I needed to leverage that privilege to advocate for my students. I was no longer a child who absorbed what was happening around me and let it mold me with bitterness. I was now a well-informed adult who believed that students like me could learn and be successful, overcoming any lingering labels with targeted support and opportunity. This shift in mindset has empowered me, replacing self-doubt and resentment with confidence and purpose.

So, let's replay that pivotal moment with Ms. Parker, applying the SCAN model.

Me: Ms. Parker, thank you for sharing your experience with bilingual education. I believe there's an opportunity here to discuss the mindset and goals of the bilingual program. While you don't teach a bilingual classroom, we share students when analyzing data and creating assessments. Additionally, during our flexible learning time, some students from the bilingual classroom come to you for specific skills, while I take some students from your class to reinforce other skills.

Ms. Parker: Oh, I'm sorry, I didn't mean to offend.

Me: I believe you, and that's why I'd like to reinforce the beliefs we've agreed on during our collaborative team time—that all our students are capable of learning at high levels. I know that's our commitment and how you feel. However, I also want to address any misconceptions within our team about students from diverse backgrounds. I think we all have something to learn about how to best support all students.

Ms. Parker: Well, OK. Do you want to meet tomorrow to talk about it during our conference time?

Me: I think we should discuss it as a team. I also believe we should learn more about the different populations we serve and the programs they're in. Maybe we can take turns as a team to highlight them and allow each of us to learn, reflect, and ask questions in a safe environment.

Ms. Parker: OK, I think that would be a good idea. Again, I'm sorry if I said something wrong.

Me: Ms. Parker, I see this as an opportunity. I don't want our blind spots to negatively impact students, and that includes me. I know there's more I need to learn.

Ms. Parker: Fair enough. Thank you.

This ending might not be an epic movie moment, but it facilitates conversations that address biases in a professional manner. This scenario creates opportunities to open dialogue, build awareness, and establish a culture of trust. Additionally, I continue to embody the characteristics of a Believer while impacting change on a grander scale. Realistically, this doesn't happen overnight; the key is consistency and continuously applying the SCAN framework.

Through the lens of a Believer, I've witnessed firsthand how a single teacher's unwavering faith in a student can shape their trajectory, igniting a passion for learning and unlocking their full potential. Ms. Semi's belief in me transcended the labels and perceptions that society often imposes, illustrating the profound influence that educators can have on shaping students' lives.

As I embarked on my own teaching career, I carried with me the lessons learned from Ms. Semi and applied them within the context of the SCAN framework. By starting with the self, I cultivated self-awareness and reflected on my biases and experiences, ensuring I approached each student with empathy and understanding. Through commitment, I remained dedicated to the principles of equity and inclusion, continuously striving to create a supportive learning environment where every student felt valued and empowered. Advocacy became my guiding principle, as I used my privilege and platform as an educator to amplify the voices of historically marginalized students and advocate for policies that promote equity and justice.

Norms also played a pivotal role in fostering a culture of trust and collaboration within my teaching teams. We navigated challenging conversations and embraced diverse perspectives with openness and respect. By incorporating the SCAN framework principles into my practice, I transformed my classroom and became an agent of change within my school community.

As a first-generation Latina navigating the complexities of the education system, I encountered both triumphs and challenges shaped by language, culture, and societal perceptions. However, my unwavering belief in my students has been grounded through self-reflection, commitment, advocacy, and calibrating my moral compass through norms. At the intersection of being a

Believer and utilizing the SCAN framework lies the potential to create a profound and lasting impact on education. It's a journey marked by continuous growth, self-reflection, and a relentless commitment to the belief that all students can learn and succeed.

References and Resources

Berk, R. A. (2017). Microaggressions trilogy: Part 3. microaggressions in the classroom. *Journal of Faculty Development, 31*(3), 95–110.

Crocker, J., & Major, B. (1989). Social stigma and self-esteem: The self-protective properties of stigma. *Psychological Review, 96*(4), 608–630.

Muhammad, A. (2018). *Transforming school culture: How to overcome staff division.* Bloomington, IN: Solution Tree Press.

Niedlich, S., Kallfass, A., Pohle, S., & Bormann, I. (2021). A comprehensive view of trust in education: Conclusions from a systematic literature review. *Review of Education, 9*(1), 124–158.

Sensoy, Ö., & DiAngelo, R. (2014). Respect differences? Challenging the common guidelines in social justice education. *Democracy and Education, 22*(2).

Sue, D. W., Capodilupo, C. M., Torino, G. C., Bucceri, J. M., Holder, A. M. B., Nadal, K. L., et al. (2007). Racial microaggressions in everyday life: Implications for clinical practice. *American Psychologist, 62*(4), 271–286.

Sue, D. W., & Spanierman, L. B. (2020). *Microaggressions in everyday life* (2nd ed.). Hoboken, NJ: Wiley.

Valencia, R. R. (1997). *The evolution of deficit thinking: Educational thought and practice.* Washington, DC: Falmer Press.

Williams, K. C. (2022). *Ruthless equity: Disrupt the status quo and ensure learning for all students.* Sharpsburg, GA: Wish in One Hand Press.

Nicole Peterson, PhD, is an educational coach with more than twenty years of experience in education as a former teacher, district instructional coach, assistant principal, and principal. Dr. Peterson completed her doctorate in K–12 Educational Leadership from Western Michigan University. She strives to help educators improve their curriculum, instruction, culture, and professional learning communities both in and outside the classroom.

To learn more about Nicole Peterson's work, visit www.linkedin.com/in/nicole-peterson-ph-d-488341249.

To book Nicole Peterson for professional development, contact pd@SolutionTree.com.

CHAPTER 6

Creating Partnerships With Parents and the Community: Reading Goals and Donut Holes

By Nicole Peterson

As a teacher, I wanted to be a leader who left a legacy, launching students into the future with passion and a joy for learning along their individual paths. It was my desire to find the perfect recipe to impact student achievement and support the whole child in education. As head chef, my teaching recipe included standards, curriculum, instruction, and assessment, among other ingredients. The quantity of these ingredients varied as I adjusted my recipe for success. I was the lead learner in the classroom, teaching students but also learning myself alongside colleagues and teammates. I asked my colleagues, "What is your recipe?" and "Do you have a secret ingredient that I have not thought of yet?" I also sought out research on how to be a better facilitator of learning. One book that had a significant impact on me was education researcher and professor John Hattie's (2008) *Visible Learning: A Synthesis of Over 800 Meta-Analyses Relating to Achievement.*

Hattie's (2008) research and synthesis of eight hundred meta-analyses influenced my thinking, pushing me to be very intentional with my time and to ensure what I was doing both inside and outside of the classroom for my students demonstrated the greatest positive impact on their learning. I dove deep into his work to understand what aspects of schooling influenced student outcomes the most—what factors had the greatest effect size. I carefully planned and incorporated influences with an effect size of over 0.50. I began my planning with the influence of promoting positive student expectations (1.44). This influence raised my curiosity and had me focusing on methods to promote a classroom culture where students embraced their own learning. Psychologist Carol Dweck's (2007) work with growth mindset added to my curiosity, as I sought ways to intentionally include activities to help students believe in their expectations for learning. I was fascinated by the multifaceted approaches Dweck (2007) shares to build self-efficacy. I asked myself and my close grade-level teammates how we could increase positive expectations with what we teach and how we model our thinking.

What I learned made me want to apologize to my students. While my recipe wasn't all wrong—I knew I was making an impact—I was not applying the most effective influences in my classroom to maximize each moment I had with my students. In considering how to adjust my recipe, I focused on parental involvement, which Hattie (2008) finds has a greater effect size (0.51) than teacher expectations (0.43). I decided to pursue this idea of how to include, involve, and engage parents. While there are many influences outside the teacher's control, there are areas of influence where they can pursue a deeper impact on student learning—parent engagement is one area. Hattie (2008) indicates that the discrepancy between parents who know how to speak the language of schooling and those who do not influences involvement level. I asked, how might I (and my school) equalize the advantage that some students have whose parents understand the academic language? How might we remove this major barrier to the home contributing to achievement?

I began reaching out and starting a conversation with my students' parents, seeking to understand what scaffolds specific to academic language I could offer between the school and home. I started with the parents with whom I had already developed relationships and a level of trust. I began with hallway conversations and phone calls, asking questions like, "If you had a magic wand, what might be some things that the school could do to help your child with literacy outside of their time in the classroom?"

In the Title I school I worked in, we were required to create *parent compacts* to outline what parents could expect from teachers and what teachers would expect from parents. The document shared how both parents and educators would receive and provide information, engage, and build trusting relationships for students' benefit. This sought to close the communication gap between home and school. The parent compact and associated buildingwide family newsletters included descriptions of our school culture. Muhammad (2018) defines culture as the beliefs, practices, behaviors, and norms of the system. These communications provided an overview of how parents could support and participate in the building's culture.

I am not naive; I did not believe that one compact—one piece of paper—was going to change the tide of school-home relationships, yet it did provide a starting point each year for communication on what our school community values. As a young teacher, I was inspired by the focus on schoolwide culture, and it forced me to examine the culture and student expectations I was creating in my classroom. I felt I had high expectations for myself and my students to demonstrate positive behaviors and interactions. I sought to create a warm and welcoming environment. Finally, I believed that *all* meant *all.* I would help all students achieve academic success. Based on the elements of what makes a positive culture as defined by researchers Kent D. Peterson (as cited in Cromwell, 2002) and Anthony Muhammad (2018), I worked with students to cocreate classroom norms, values, beliefs, rituals, ceremonies, symbols, and cocreated and shared stories. As with the schoolwide effort, the next step of my educational journey was to find ways to have parents involved in creating the classroom culture. This is how the program Reading Goals and Donut Holes began, and it necessitated an examination of the difference between parental involvement and parental engagement in the classroom.

Parental Involvement Versus Engagement

Take a moment to reflect on the ways parents have traditionally interacted in your classroom and larger school. We had parents who were involved—helping in the classroom by cutting out student materials, creating bulletin boards, packing weekly reading materials, and creating packets of homework and graded student work to send home. We had parents visiting classrooms to listen to kids read or helping with a craft center. We also had an involved parent-teacher organization that supported classroom party planning, carnivals, and other school activities. We were thrilled with this involvement in our school. Students were observing parents and teachers working together. The system certainly fostered parent involvement; however, we wondered how we might improve parental engagement focused on academics. For such engagement, we envisioned students experiencing similar academic language, both at home and at school, and engaging with parents about reading, writing, and arithmetic. We wanted students to hear parents and teachers engaging in conversation about academics.

Through a review of classroom, grade-level, and building data, we found that students were decoding text with increasing accuracy. We also discovered that they were challenged to apply comprehension strategies to what they had read. We collaboratively set goals to increase read-aloud and think-aloud time. We focused on modeling our thinking for students to uncover the inner thought process and conversational voice that takes place when reading and speaking. We set goals focusing on accountable talk to include substantive conversation related to what students were reading. During reading instruction and independent practice, students were asked to annotate their text with sticky notes and demonstrate how they were monitoring their comprehension and applying metacognition.

The staff engaged in a book study using *7 Keys to Comprehension: How to Help Your Kids Read It and Get It!* (Zimmermann & Hutchins, 2003). After reading the book and incorporating instructional shifts in our curriculum, I wrote a grant proposal to our local education association for the purchase of twenty books to loan to families to read and return intending to bring parents into an interactive conversation about literacy. The book was written for parents and teachers, so we felt confident that it would be a productive book for conversation and would not overwhelm those not directly in the education field.

After the grant was approved, we began a book club with the parent-teacher organization. We discussed the book and collected takeaways that the parent group had taken from reading the material. We asked for their suggestions on how to set up a parent program that was inviting, inclusive, and productive in a safe, nonthreatening environment. We created a book trailer with clips of our students at work to share with parents how they could read the book *with* us. Parents visited the school office to pick up a loaned copy, or we sent one home with their student. As the books were returned, a member of our committee called the parents to gather their reactions to the book. We continued this process, loaning out books and then calling families, for approximately six months. Our goal was to create a safe environment for parent learning within the school, so after the six-month span of collecting data, our committee processed the parent feedback and reactions. Two of the greatest findings included (1) parents wanted to be an active participant in their child's learning with the vocabulary that we were using during the school day, and (2) parents felt that when resources were modeled and provided for and with them, they would be more likely to use them at home. We then decided it was time to implement a program to bring parents into the school and provide them with resources and positive experiences.

The next level of parent engagement involved investment in three Cs: (1) collaborating, (2) communicating, and (3) celebrating with parents. Our school had embraced the implementation of common literacy vocabulary to support reading comprehension across all grade levels, later learning that educational researcher, speaker, and author Robert J. Marzano (2010) was working on the importance of direct academic vocabulary instruction. We wanted to promote a culture that included the school-home connection of common vocabulary and strategies for students. We created Reading Goals and Donut Holes with the intention to bring together Hattie's (2008) learning about student positive expectation and parental engagement with Marzano's (2010) work with direct teaching of literacy-based academic language to increase the likelihood of student learning success. We knew these were lofty goals, but we were up for the challenge. Our committee then wrote another grant proposal for the funds needed to kick off the program's first year.

Due to the success of both staff and parent participation in the study with the book *The 7 Keys to Comprehension* (Zimmermann & Hutchins, 2003) and our early findings from parents, our committee thought that continuing to use this text would be the perfect way to further engage parents in a community-based learning experience. The text is organized in chapters that each focus on one comprehension strategy: creating mental images, using background knowledge to make connections, asking questions, making inferences, determining what is most important, synthesizing, and using fix-up strategies. We decided that we would make an event out of each strategy and have parents learn, experience, and practice the strategy with their child, using a gradual release of responsibility to the parents. Each event would be set up in the same format: The presenter models (I do); the presenter, parents, and students do it together (we do); and the parent and child do it together (they do). Then the parent and child would be given a reminder gift on how to do it together at home (independent; Pearson & Gallagher, 1983).

As you read this chapter, keep an open mind about how you might apply this program format to meet your community's needs. You might determine another book is a better fit for your community. Our goal was to share with parents how to name comprehension strategies when they were reading to their children or listening to them read. Our intention was to facilitate ways to make the strategies visible for parents. This book best matched our goals. The goals of your district or building will be different. I encourage you to take this model and apply the framework to meet your needs.

Reading Goals and Donut Holes

The learning outcomes we sought to reach with the Reading Goals and Donut Holes program were as follows.

- Educators will:
    - Invite parents to join in learning through role play and practice with their child
    - Support the growth and potential of positive parental mindsets
    - Model healthy and high expectations for all learners
    - Model how to ask and respond to children in academic interactions
    - Create shared vocabulary with scaffolded supports for students and parents
- Parents will:
    - Experience that they are not alone in the journey of parenting
    - Experience the wonder of learning and of their child's will to grow
    - Celebrate in the joy of their child's success
    - Understand that mistakes are a part of learning and on-time feedback supports positive literacy behaviors
    - Build positive relationships with the school and with other parents

We created Reading Goals and Donut Holes as a before-school program to bring parents, teachers, and students together. We opened our classrooms for families to come into school to read books with their students once per month. Over time, participation grew so much that we moved sessions to a larger space in the school.

The program started at 8:00 a.m.; parents and students helped themselves to donuts, juice, and coffee before moving into the classrooms where there were book bins with books of all levels representing many topics. These were one-sit books that could fully engage both the parent and the child in the story's continuity. We only had a dedicated twenty-five minutes of reading time with both parent and child together, so the books that we provided needed to be short, quick reads.

We designed seven sessions—one for each strategy outlined in *The 7 Keys of Comprehension*. When parents entered, the comprehension strategy for that session was posted on the board. For example, our first session was focused on making mental images. So, we had a poster on the board that said, "Readers make a movie in their mind of what is happening in the story as they read it. When you are reading today, share with your child the movie or images that you are thinking about when you hear the words from the author. Do this at the end of each page or couple of pages." Here are other examples of our calls to action related to the strategies of using background knowledge to make connections, asking questions, making inferences, determining what is most important, synthesizing, and using fix-up strategies (Zimmermann & Hutchins, 2003).

- Before turning the page, ask, "What does the author want me to know?" (determining what is important)
- Turn to your child or parent and ask them, "What does this story remind you of?" (using background knowledge to make a connection)
- Before turning the page, ask, "What are one or two sentences that share what is happening in the story?" (synthesizing)

Once parents and students were settled with their books, we gathered everyone's attention to model the call-to-action strategy using a large book. We kept the modeling to less than three minutes because we wanted families to practice the skill, not hear a lecture. After modeling the process and the name of the strategy, parents were encouraged to practice the strategy with their child. For the next ten to fifteen minutes, teachers circulated the room observing and making themselves available to parents or students who had questions. We were mindful to keep an appropriate distance so that families felt comfortable trying out this strategy without fear of doing it wrong or being judged or criticized. Our goal was to create a safe place for all families to spend time immersed in literacy.

At 8:25 a.m., students cleaned up and headed outside for morning recess. This left eight to ten minutes to review and model the call-to-action strategy again with the parents, sharing its importance related to literacy, and provide them with a takeaway on how to use the strategy at home. It was also important for us to hear from families. Initially, parents were reluctant to share their experiences, comments, or questions. We utilized a variety of nonthreatening methods for participation; one week we used a chalk talk activity where we put a piece of chart paper on each table. Three to six parents sat at a table and were asked to quietly write their thoughts or reactions to the experience. The following are sample prompts that may have been included.

- This helped me . . .
- I noticed my child . . .
- This strategy is helpful because . . .

Each chart paper was then collected and randomly posted at the front of the room. The presenter read the various responses. This format allowed all voices to be heard, and the comments remained anonymous. We then began whole-group discussion; parents could expand on their own thought or the thoughts of others.

Sentence prompts, such as those in figure 6.1, were provided so parents could model the academic language teachers use in the classroom for making a prediction, asking a question, making a comment, and making a connection.

The following materials we used made Reading Goals and Donut Holes successful.

- One-sit books for various readability levels and interests
- Chart paper and an anchor sheet with the call to action for parents
- Projection system to model strategy for students and families
- Copies of sentence stems on tables as handouts (in English, Spanish, and so on, to match the participants' language or languages)
- Refreshments and supplies (paper products, donut holes, or another item that connects with your community, such as a food from their country)
- Sign-in page for student and parent names
- Copies of *7 Keys to Comprehension* (or whatever book your school uses that connects with the focus of your event)

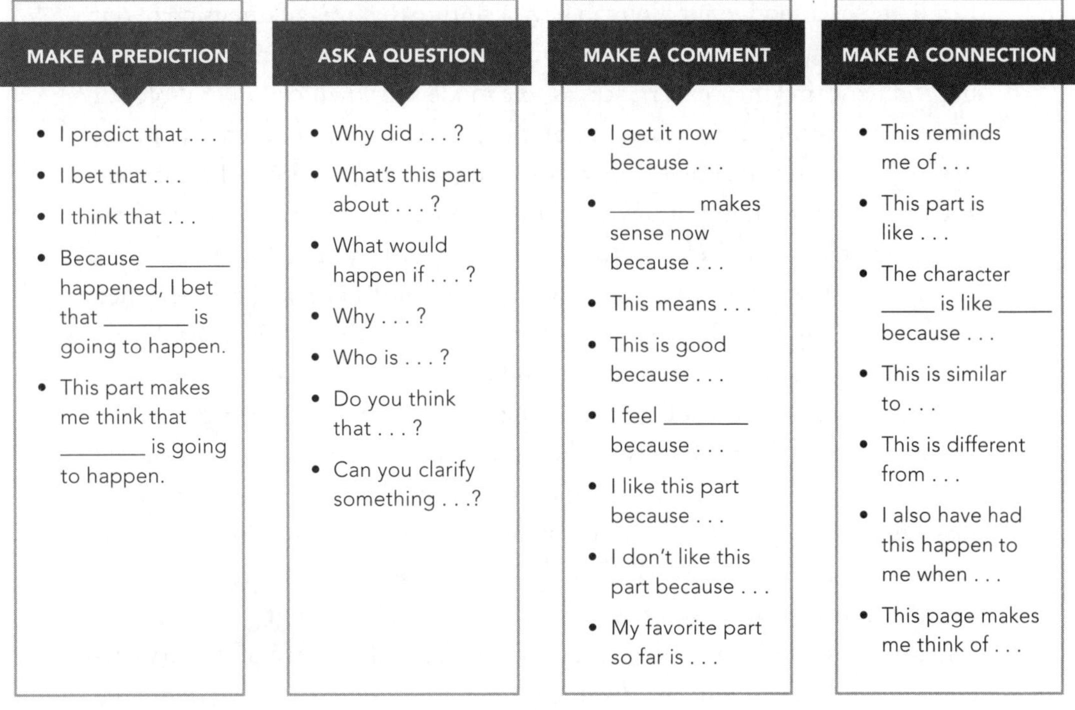

Figure 6.1: Reading prompts for parents to model.

- Item to give away (such as magnets or bookmarks printed with a phrase connected to the reading like, *Thinking about my reading*)

In planning how to implement a program like Reading Goals and Donut Holes to your learning environment, it is important to be mindful about making the structure sustainable. Ask the following questions.

- How can I set family at the center of the conversation when planning?
- How can I provide the most equitable access to this experience?
- How can I include responsiveness to families' cultural and linguistic needs?
- How might I set up the environment and information to build on the strengths of the cultures my students represent?

As we prepared for Reading Goals and Donut Holes sessions, we were mindful and intentional about the words and stories used with parents. Educational researcher and author Michael Fullan (2006) reminds us that we must apply inclusive language to fully honor people's dignity and respect. We wanted

Reading Goals and Donut Holes to have a culture that was an extension of our classrooms. Our desire was for parents to thrive in a safe environment, preserving and honoring their experiences as role models for their children. Professor Peter H. Johnston (2004) shares in his book *Choice Words* how educators can position students and families differently depending on the choice of vocabulary and the narrative they create. Word choice influences every exchange and how people interact within relationships: "Language has content, but it also bears information about the speaker and how they view the listener and their assumed relationship" (Johnston, 2004, p. 5). For example, inviting parents has a very different tone than telling them and will influence how they receive information. Consider if you said the following: "Parents, we invite you to incorporate this strategy when reading with your children at home" versus "Parents, you should be using this strategy." The word choice changes the tone and how the message may be received. Saying, "Creating fun and calming reading habits with your child every night supports a lifelong love for literacy" will be received better than, "Parents, we need you to work with your child on reading every night." The first example focuses on the fun of reading and how it builds a parent-child relationship, supporting the student, not the teacher. Therefore, we chose our language carefully.

We also leaned into the art of storytelling and narratives during our engagement with parents and the community. Fullan (2006) and professor John P. Kotter (2012) both share in their research that, to help people change their habits, it is necessary to speak to their feelings. Storytelling connects with people in ways that influence their emotions, not just their thinking. I was mindful to launch every Reading Goals and Donut Holes with a story, poem, or experience that parents could connect with. I prepared parents who were planning to attend by calling them and letting them know to be ready with a story or experience to share with other parents. The sharing from one parent prompted other adults to spontaneously share their own connected experiences. Narratives are portals into personal and collective interpretive processing and to understanding others' perspectives (Ravitch, 2020). We believed that parents' stories, experiences, and connections needed to be shared with others, so we were intentional of creating time and space within the Reading Goals and Donut Holes sessions for this purpose. We also created a space in our feedback forms for parents to share their experiences, connections, and reflections with us.

Touchpoints for Effective School-Family-Community Partnerships

Research scientist and professor Joyce L. Epstein and colleagues (2018) share four directions for organizing and conducting more effective school, family, and community partnerships that contribute to student success. The first measure is to include teamwork for program development. Retrospectively, we had intentionally moved through increasing broader groups of influence in our community to build teamwork for development. We started with educators, and then we included the parent-teacher organization, and, finally, families who volunteered to read the book and provide feedback.

The second area Epstein and colleagues (2018) focus on is creating goal-linked partnership activities. We were clear with our goals to create a shared experience with families and transparent and transportable vocabulary between home and school.

The third area stresses the importance of equity in outreach to all families. We applied the lens of equitable experiences and access for parents. We brainstormed and worked with our key communicators of various populations. We asked questions about obstacles to our work and how we could provide access for all. I wish I could say that we were able to connect with all families, but I can't; however, our conscious efforts did create access for more than we thought possible during the initial planning stages. We worked to create responsive communication structures that allowed parents to engage in a manner that was convenient for them. We were flexible to allow for families with limited time or resources to gain the information they missed from the actual event. We sent information home in children's backpacks to families in printed newsletters (in both Spanish and English), and we used the postal service to mail targeted communication to families that we had identified had students with academic performance below 65 percent of standard expectation. We also sent emails in both languages. These areas were just the start of forming equity in outreach. I recommend focusing on making equitable access a part of the goal and then working strategically to do a few of the action steps very well. After, you can then build on the successes and grow the circles of influence.

The final area is the evaluation of program quality and results of partnership activists. We were clear on our learning outcomes and tight on our success criteria. We surveyed parents at the end of each school year to gather data related to our learning outcomes and success criteria. The survey questions included, but were not limited to, the following.

- How many of the seven sessions did you attend this school year?
- What were the reasons you returned for another session?
- What was your experience in three to five words?
- Would you recommend this program to other parents?
- What did you notice about this time spent with your child?
- How might we improve this program?

The program had an impact on the unique and influential parent-child relationship, which is critical to adolescents' physical and mental development (Zeigler-Hill & Shackelford, 2020). One example of a collected data point showed that 92 percent of participating families responded that Reading Goals and Donut Holes created bonding time with their children. Students were able to showcase for their parents the school environment and choose literature to build a positive literacy experience. In the safety and structure of the program, we observed students sitting on their parents' laps or elbow to elbow reading books. We used our district website and building-level newsletter communications to share the data we collected and to celebrate the success. We shared quantitative data—numbers, graphs, and demographics of participants. We also celebrated the qualitative data that was collected with our findings and anecdotal testimonies shared by both students and parents. Finally, I attended and presented at a couple local conferences on Reading Goals and Donut Holes so that we could celebrate our success for the district, share the process with other districts, and offer suggestions on how to make the framework of this parental engagement activity meaningful.

A Culture of Learning in the Home

I was listening to a webinar hosted by educator and author William Ferriter (2023), and he asked the question, "What is the doability and importance of this work?" If it does not feel doable or important, the work will not get done. The importance of parental involvement and engagement is so well-established that it stands as one of the most agreed-on principles in education. Hattie (2022) demonstrates that parental involvement has an effect size of 0.51. Parental engagement supports higher grades, test scores, and increased school attendance, and students display higher educational desires with an effect size of 0.42. This also includes improved social competencies and emotional health including self-confidence and positive attitudes (Jung & Zhang, 2016; Wong & Hughes, 2006). Parent expectations and what they believe about their child's potential has an effect size of 0.7, which is double the effect of teacher expectations. Therefore, when we look at a program that supports the parent and includes teacher expertise (0.9), the combined effect of our work is critical. This work is too important to do alone.

We also know that when teachers share in the work by planning and implementing together, the heavy burden becomes more doable. Hattie's (2023) research supports that collective teacher efficacy has an effect size of 1.57—the collective belief that not only am I a Believer, but we are Believers together.

Hattie and Hattie (2022) share four critical areas of focus for parents as they cultivate a culture of learning in the home: (1) communicate effectively with teachers, (2) be the "first learner" and demonstrate openness to new ideas and thinking, (3) choose the right school for your child, and (4) promote the language of learning. Reading Goals and Donut Holes, in process and practice, assisted parents in forming visible pathways for learning with educators for students. How might these ideas fit into the vision of your parent engagement planning?

Conclusion

I have interviewed hundreds of potential teachers during my sixteen years as an elementary administrator. When asked, "Why did you go into teaching?" the answer was usually something like, "A teacher made a difference in my life, and I want to give back in a similar way," "I love children," or "I come from a family of educators." Candidates spoke of an inner calling, motivation, and drive toward teaching and learning. Most people go into teaching because they believe in their potential to make a difference. When asked about their thoughts on relationships with parents, however, the responses were less precise—usually that these relationships were essential, but the "how to" was not as clear. There was a crevasse between communicating the importance of engaging families and then doing something about it. As educators, we are challenged to bring parents into the conversation and the work we do in schools. Programs like Reading Goals and Donut Holes bring parents and families into the school culture, increasing the number of Believers who support students.

References and Resources

Cromwell, S. (2002). Is your school culture toxic or positive? *Education World, 6*(2). Accessed at www.educationworld.com/a_admin/admin/admin275.shtml on March 2, 2017.

Dweck, C. S. (2007). *Mindset: The new psychology of success.* New York: Ballantine Books.

Epstein, J. L., Sanders, M. G., Sheldon, S. B., Simon, B. S., Salinas, K. C., Jansorn, N. R., et al. (2018). *School, family, and community partnerships: Your handbook for action* (4th ed.). Thousand Oaks, CA: Corwin Press.

Ferriter, W. (2023, December). *Using AI tools to facilitate better teaching and learnings* [Webinar]. Bloomington, IN: Solution Tree Press.

Fullan, M. (2006). *Turnaround leadership.* San Francisco: Jossey-Bass.

Germeroth, C. (2022, July 26). *Marzano Research leads family engagement framework development in Colorado.* Accessed at https://marzanoresearch.com/marzano-research-leads-family-engagement-framework-development-in-colorado on April 25, 2024.

Hamilton, A., Reeves, D. B., Clinton, J. M., & Hattie, J. (2022). *Building to impact: The 5D implementation playbook for educators.* Thousand Oaks, CA: Corwin Press.

Harrison Berg, J. (2020). Leading together/Teams to the rescue. *Educational Leadership, 78*(2), 78–79.

Hattie, J. (2008). *Visible learning: A synthesis of over 800 meta-analyses relating to achievement* (1st ed.). New York: Routledge.

Hattie, J. (2012). *Visible learning for teachers: Maximizing impact on learning.* New York: Routledge.

Hattie, J. (2023). *Visible learning: The sequel. A synthesis of over 2,100 meta-analyses relating to achievement.* New York: Routledge.

Hattie, J., & Hattie, K. (2022). *10 steps to develop great learners: Visible learning for parents.* New York: Routledge.

Johnston, P. H. (2004). *Choice words: How our language affects children's learning.* Portland, ME: Stenhouse Publishers.

Jung, E., & Zhang, Y. (2016). Parental involvement, children's aspirations, and achievement in new immigrant families. *The Journal of Educational Research, 109,* 333–350. https://doi.org/10.1080/00220671.2014.959112

Kanter, R. M. (2004). *Confidence: How winning and losing streaks begin and end.* New York: Crown Business.

Kotter, J. P. (2012). *Leading change.* Boston: Harvard Business Review Press

Marzano, R. J. (2010). *Teaching basic and advanced vocabulary: A framework for direct instruction.* Boston: Heinle.

McFalone, D. (2019). *Uncommon leadership: Live well, lead strong for courage and integrity.* Lanham, MD: Rowman & Littlefield.

Muhammad, A. (2018). *Transforming school culture: How to overcome staff division* (2nd ed.). Bloomington, IN: Solution Tree Press.

Pearson, P. D., & Gallagher, M. (1983). The instruction of reading comprehension. *Contemporary Educational Psychology*, *8*(3), 317–344. https://doi.org/10.1016/0361-476X(83)90019-X

Quezada, R. L., Alexandrowicz, V., & Molina, S. C. (2015). *Family, school, community engagement and partnerships: Theory and best practices.* New York: Routledge.

Ravitch, S. M. (2020). Flux leadership: Leading for justice and peace in and beyond COVID-19. *Perspectives on Urban Education*, *18*(1), 1–31.

Tye, N. (2023). Engaging families after Covid: Reconnecting in the classroom. *PDS Partners: Bridging Research to Practice*, *18*(1), 61–69. https://doi.org/10.1108/PDSP-01-2023-0003

Wheatley, M. J. (2007). *Find our way: Leadership for an uncertain time.* Oakland, CA: Berrett-Koehler.

Wong, S. W., & Hughes, J. N. (2006). Ethnicity and language contributions to dimensions of parent involvement. *School Psychology Review*, *35*(4), 645–662.

Zeigler-Hill, V., and Shackelford, T. K. (2020). *Encyclopedia of personality and individual differences.* Switzerland: Springer, 3433–3435. https://doi.org/10.1007/978-3-319-24612-3

Zimmermann, S., & Hutchins, C. (2003). *7 keys to comprehension: How to help your kids read it and get it!* New York: Three Rivers Press.

Bo Ryan is principal of the Ana Grace Academy of the Arts Middle Magnet School in Bloomfield, Connecticut. He has led two different schools to Model PLC at Work certification: Woodside Intermediate School in 2012 and Greater Hartford Academy of the Arts Middle School in 2016, just four years after it opened in a factory in the middle of a city. In addition, he led Ana Grace Academy to HRS (High Reliability Schools) Level 4.

Bo has worked in education since 1994, having served as a teacher, coach, director, adjunct professor, principal, author, and consultant. He is author of *The Brilliance in the Building: Effecting Change in Urban Schools With the PLC at Work Process*, a collection of all his experience teaching and learning in urban schools over two decades.

To book Bo Ryan for professional development, contact pd@SolutionTree.com.

CHAPTER 7

Collaborating for Classroom Culture: Doing the Right Work

By Bo Ryan

Educators work hard in schools every day—there is no question about that. But they need to be doing the *right work*—the work that is likely to impact student and staff learning. With well-designed plans that show a sense of urgency and systems change, educators can move in the right direction toward using actionable data immediately in their classrooms to improve student learning and their instruction. This type of systemic change can be a challenge for educational leaders to plan and difficult for teachers to accept and understand—especially when a staff has been "doing education" the same way for years. Why should they change now? Staff might also lack the professional knowledge to focus on the right work—they have the will but not the skill. Other times, schools don't know what the right work looks like.

The right work in schools is work that focuses on student and staff learning and is also equitable. *Equity* means that "all students—regardless of race, ethnicity, family income, zip code—are all entitled to excellent educational opportunities and the resources and supports they need to succeed in school" (Montell, 2023). Educational experts Robert Marzano, Phillip B. Warrick, Cameron L. Rains, and Richard DuFour (2018) state that educators who strive for such excellence must do the following.

> Take steps to ensure that all students not only have equal access to but also acquire the knowledge, skills, and dispositions that will prepare them for the future. These institutions that were created to sort and select students based on their perceived abilities, socioeconomic status, and likely career now are called on to ensure every student graduates from high school with the high levels of learning necessary for success in college or other avenues of postsecondary training. In short, schools cannot become excellent unless they commit to equity as well. (p. 1)

The Professional Learning Communities at Work® (PLC at Work) process (DuFour, DuFour, Eaker, Many, Mattos, & Muhammad, 2024) provides a clear plan to ensure educators do the right work. In a PLC, educators "do more than give students the chance to learn—they must align their practices to promote learning" (DuFour et al., p. 63). The mission statements of many PLC districts and schools include the words "learning for all," which is the embodiment of equity (Muhammad, 2024).

A Process to Ensure the Right Work

The solution for teams to focus on the right work is the PLC process with its three big ideas: (1) a focus on learning, (2) collaboration and collective responsibility, and (3) a results orientation (DuFour et al., 2024). The research on student achievement in schools using the PLC process is well-documented (Cottingham, Hough, & Myung, 2023; Hanson et al., 2021; Read On Arizona, 2024; Solution Tree, 2024a–c). Richard DuFour, Rebecca DuFour, Robert Eaker, Mike Mattos, and Anthony Muhammad (2021) state that "the only hope for creating schools that are continuously improving their capacity to raise student achievement is to establish the expectation that educators must engage in the ongoing study and constant practice in the field" (p. 11). The PLC process provides that hope, but it must be implemented the right way—with collaborative teams of teachers who utilize time embedded in the weekly schedule to meet; plan and implement a guaranteed and viable curriculum; create, administer, and score common formative assessments; and use the results from the data to take action to ensure students learn and instruction improves. Teacher teams in a PLC constantly monitor their students and their plans, revising plans in real time as needed.

The PLC process, with its focus on teacher and student learning, team collaboration, and student results is a tool for building a healthy school culture.

Anthony Muhammad (2018) notes that *culture* is how we behave; it is "the way we do things around here" (Gruenert & Whitaker, 2015, p. 10). Muhammad (2018) defines a healthy school culture as a place where:

> - Educators have an unwavering belief in the ability of all their students to achieve success, and they pass that belief on to others in overt and covert ways.
> - Educators create policies and procedures and adopt practices that support their belief in every student's ability (p. 21).

The opposite of a healthy school culture is a toxic school culture, which Muhammad (2018) describes as when:

> - Educators believe that student success is based on students' level of concern, attentiveness, prior knowledge, and willingness to comply with the demands of the school, and they articulate that belief in overt and covert ways.
> - Educators create policies and procedures and adopt practices that support their belief in the impossibility of universal achievement. (p. 21)

Muhammad (2018) states that to make substantive improvements in schools it will take "deep reflection on our individual and collective behaviors and creating conditions that allow us to improve our practices and behaviors" (p. 20). As teachers, if we care deeply about every student, then we will try to do everything possible to help every student achieve at a high level. That means making shifts in the way we work. The PLC process requires that teachers make these shifts for improvement to become a reality. The biggest shift in the work of teachers in PLC is from teachers working in isolation to teachers working as part of collaborative teams (DuFour et al., 2024).

A Shift From Isolation to Collaboration

A major change in schools that function as PLCs is to shift from a culture of isolation to a culture of collaboration. A *collaborative team* is a group of educators who meet on a regular basis to focus on the right work to improve student and staff learning (DuFour et al., 2024). As Muhammad (2018) notes, "The powerful paradigm that we are much more effective together than we are separately drives the entire PLC process" (p. 132).

Research supports the power of using collaborative teams rather than the practice of teachers working in isolation (Carroll, 2009; Chenoweth, 2009;

Hattie, 2015; Many & Sparks-Many, 2015). In particular, DuFour and colleagues (2024) describe nine shifts in the work of teachers in a traditional system of isolation to collaboration in a PLC (table 7.1).

Table 7.1: The Shift in the Work of Teachers From Isolation to Collaboration

From Isolation . . .	To Collaboration
From each teacher clarifying what students must learn . . .	To collaborative teams building shared knowledge and understanding about essential learning
From each teacher assigning priority to different learning standards . . .	To collaborative teams establishing the priority of respective learning standards
From each teacher determining the pacing of the curriculum . . .	To collaborative teams of teachers agreeing on common pacing
From individual teachers attempting to discover ways to improve results . . .	To collaborative teams of teachers helping each other improve
From privatization of practice . . .	To open sharing of practice
From decisions made on the basis of individual preferences . . .	To decisions made collectively by building shared knowledge of best practice
From "collaboration lite," collaboration on matters unrelated to student achievement, . . .	To collaboration explicitly focused on issues and questions that most impact student achievement
From an assumption that these are "my students, those are your students" . . .	To an assumption that these are "our students"

Source: DuFour et al., 2024.

Collaboration builds *collective teacher efficacy*, which is a team's shared belief that members can collectively impact student learning and take action to do so. In her book *Collective Efficacy: How Educators' Beliefs Impact Student Learning*, Jenni Donohoo (2017) finds that fostering collective teacher efficacy should be at the forefront of planned strategic effort in all schools, and, given its effect on student achievement, it should be a top priority for everyone in education.

Collaboration provides teachers with access to a built-in support systems. There should be a sense of urgency for creating collaborative teams in all schools, but it is especially important in urban schools, where teachers need access to support systems to handle the daily stressors of the job. A significant problem in urban education is how many teachers leave the profession (Love, 2021). Underserved schools lose 20 percent of their faculty each year (NYU Steinhardt School of Culture, Education, and Human Development, 2018). Teachers reasons for leaving include ineffective leadership, subpar working conditions, and lack of peer support (NYU Steinhardt School of Culture, Education, and Human Development, 2018). "Stress and burnout are pervasive among public school teachers and amplified in urban schools, where job demands are often high and resources low" (Bottiani, Duran, Pas, & Bradshaw, 2019). The most important route to promote a healthy work environment for teachers is with high levels of collegiality (Ouellette et al., 2018). Teachers who have more connection with colleagues and a sense of self-efficacy report lower stress and burnout (Bottiani, et al., 2019). When teachers collaborate with team members, colleagues, and administrators, they feel a greater sense of community within their school, which creates a positive teaching and learning environment for both staff and students (Love, 2021).

In a PLC, teachers engage in work in collaborative teams to build shared knowledge (DuFour et al., 2024). The culture shifts from a focus on *teaching* to a focus on *learning*, and from an emphasis on what was *taught* to a fixation on what students *learned* (DuFour et al., 2024). In their collaborative teams, teachers in a PLC engage in a cycle of continuous improvement where they answer four critical questions of a PLC (DuFour et al., 2024).

1. What knowledge, skills, and dispositions should every student acquire as a result of this unit, this course, or this grade level?
2. How will we know when each student has acquired the essential knowledge and skills?
3. How will we respond when some students do not learn?
4. How will we extend the learning for students who are already proficient? (p. 44)

When answering critical question one, grade-level or subject-area teams of teachers determine what every student should know and be able to do; this ensures students across classes experience a guaranteed and viable curriculum. A *guaranteed and viable curriculum* (Marzano, 2003) is one that provides students with "access to the same curriculum content in a specific course and at a specific grade level, regardless of their assigned teacher; and teachers can teach this curriculum in the amount of instructional time provided" (Marzano, Warrick, Rains, & DuFour, 2018, p. 7).

When teacher teams answer the second critical question of a PLC, they are determining how they will collectively know that each student has learned what the team has determined they must learn. This means team members must work together to create, administer, and score common formative assessments—assessments *for* learning.

To answer the third and fourth critical questions—How will we respond when students don't learn and how will we extend their learning when they do?—collaborative teams meet and discuss the data from the common formative assessments to take action by reflecting on and improving instruction and creating a plan to give students more time and support, intervention, and extension.

This cycle of learning within collaborative teams in a PLC can be called many things—a learning cycle (Kramer & Schuhl, 2017; 2023), a PDSA (plan, do, study, act) cycle (Bailey & Jacicik, 2023), a team teaching-assessing cycle (Buffum, Mattos, & Malone, 2018), a coaching cycle (Sweeney & Harris, 2020), a learning block (Ryan, 2023). Regardless of what educational experts may call it, the cycle consists of planning, teaching, assessing, and using the results to take action.

In a PLC, there are elements that are tight (non-negotiable) and elements that are loose (educators have discretion with implementation). Collaboration is a tight in a PLC, and the work of teams—answering the four critical questions—is also non-negotiable. The work of strong collaborative teams in a PLC is where healthy culture building takes place. In my career as an educator and educational consultant, I have learned much about the constant change that happens in schools: school leaders change; staff members change; federal, state, and district policies change; students change; and communities change. The tight practices in a PLC do not change, and these provide a calm against the storm that changes can bring.

The following sections provide a look into the collaborative cycle of inquiry in a PLC where teams answer the four critical questions to ensure a guaranteed and viable curriculum, assess student learning, and use the results to make data-driven decisions about instruction. To access more detailed information about the processes and tools in the following sections, see *The Brilliance in the Building: Effecting Change in Urban Schools With the PLC at Work Process* (Ryan,

2023), as well as the critical foundational text *Learning by Doing: A Handbook for Professional Learning Communities at Work* (DuFour et al., 2024).

Ensuring a Guaranteed and Viable Curriculum

One of the most important parts of the right work is to plan and ensure a guaranteed and viable curriculum; all students must have access to the grade-level standards. Austin Buffum, Mike Mattos, and Janet Malone (2018) state that "once [teams] determine these critical standards, the school must guarantee that teachers teach them to students as part of their core instruction" (p. 159). This includes more than just planning the curriculum by choosing the targeted standards; it also includes discussions about pacing of the learning cycle, creating an instructional plan, and designing grade-level assignments. Robert Marzano (2003), in his research of effective schools, states that a guaranteed and viable curriculum is the number one strategy high reliability schools have in common (Marzano et al., 2018). Also critical is that there is adequate time to teach the curriculum, thus making it viable (Bailey & Jacicik, 2023; Marzano et al., 2018).

This section shares tools collaborative teams in PLCs can use to plan and create a guaranteed and viable curriculum. Figure 7.1 (page 108) shows the first two steps.

- Review and discuss the priority standards using the REAL criteria (Ainsworth, 2003): readiness, endurance, assessment, and leverage. Does the standard provide students with the skills and knowledge to succeed in the next grade level or class? Are the skills and knowledge useful beyond the specific unit of study? Will the standard be the focus of assessment on national, state, province, or local exam? Does the standard give students skills and knowledge across multiple disciplines?
- Unwrap the standards into learning targets. Teams build shared knowledge to create learning targets to share with students. Teams develop the learning progression by numbering the standards from simpler to more complex concepts and skills. They discuss the needed learning goals not directly in the standard. They identify learning targets by writing each verb (skill) and noun (concept) combination as separate learning targets. Each learning target must break down each standard into specific skills and knowledge students need to learn to master the standard, be measurable, and be written using *I can* statements that clearly explain in student-friendly language what the students will learn.

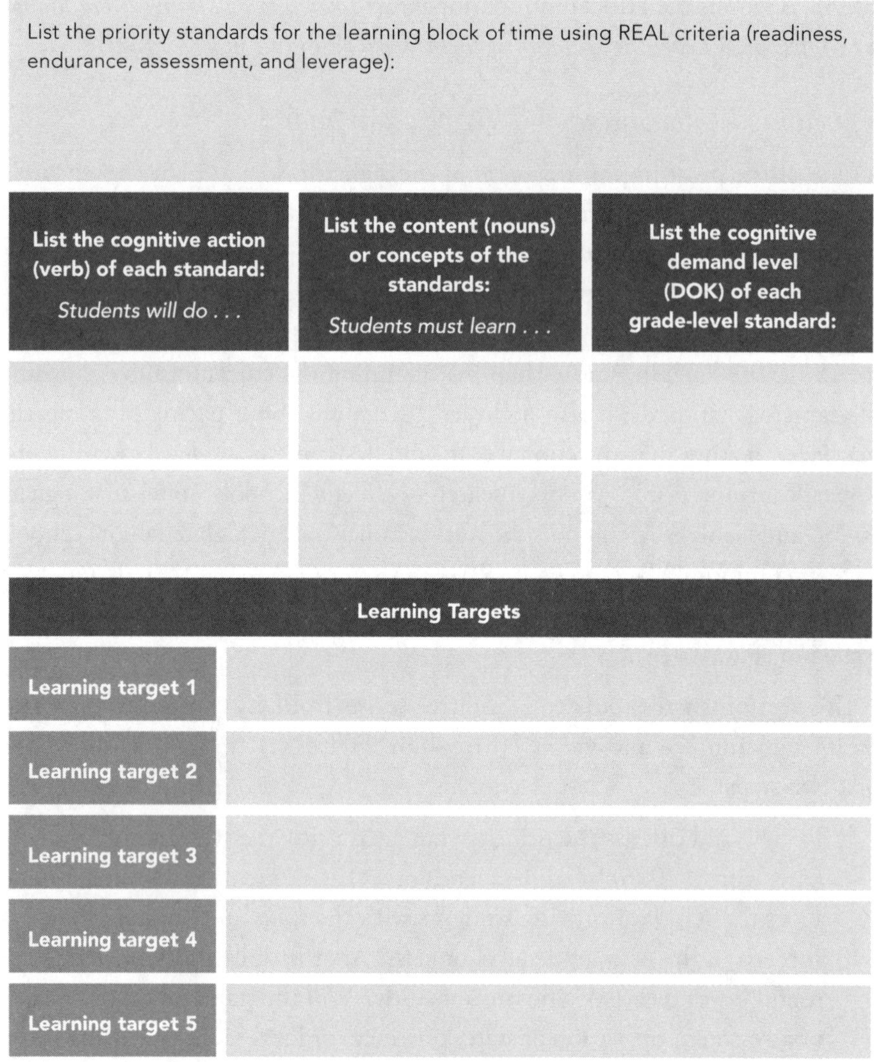

List the priority standards for the learning block of time using REAL criteria (readiness, endurance, assessment, and leverage):

List the cognitive action (verb) of each standard: *Students will do . . .*	List the content (nouns) or concepts of the standards: *Students must learn . . .*	List the cognitive demand level (DOK) of each grade-level standard:

Learning Targets	
Learning target 1	
Learning target 2	
Learning target 3	
Learning target 4	
Learning target 5	

Source: Depka, 2017; Hess, K., 2013; Kramer & Schuhl, 2017.

Figure 7.1: Determining priority standards for ensuring a guaranteed and viable curriculum.

Visit ***go.SolutionTree.com/schoolimprovement*** *for a free reproducible version of this figure.*

Teams can also take the work a step farther by taking the team meeting to the classroom using learning scales, a version of Marzano's (2020) proficiency scales. This process not only allows teams to build absolute clarity on the standards but also on the district's curriculum expectations. Figure 7.2 shows the process for creating learning scales.

Learning Target	Mastery of Standard *(With Success Criteria)*	Approaching Standard *(With Prerequisite Skills and Vocabulary)*	Exceeding Standard *(Thinking Beyond Mastery)*	Scaffolds for the Learning Targets and Teaching Tips
Learning target 1				
Learning target 2				
Learning target 3				

Source: *Depka, 2017; Hess, K., 2013; Kramer & Schuhl, 2017.*

Figure 7.2: Learning scales for mastery of standards.

*Visit **go.SolutionTree.com/schoolimprovement** for a free reproducible version of this figure.*

- Write the learning target for mastery of standards.
- Write success criteria for mastery. What does good work look like? Include exemplars.
    - Determine vocabulary, simple procedures, and prerequisite content.
    - Discuss thinking beyond mastery with examples of exceeding mastery.
    - Discuss scaffolds for each target and teaching tips.

The learning scales process in figure 7.2 can transition from the meeting to the classroom when teachers post the learning scales in the classroom and use it as an instructional tool. Students will know their level of performance and have the ability to set goals, self-grade, and chart their progress. In addition to creating learning scales to impact instruction, teams also create a plan for instruction. Teams can use a simple tool like the one in figure 7.3 to talk about how they plan on teaching during the cycle of learning.

Grade-Level Assignments Aligned to Priority Standards
How can we ensure all students have access to high-quality assignments that align to the learning targets?
Can we add any culturally relevant resources?
What instructional strategies work best with this unit?
How will you and the students use learning scales to monitor learning?
Which vocabulary words will you assess and teach using direct instruction during this cycle of learning?

Source: Depka, 2017; Hess, K., 2013; Kramer & Schuhl, 2017.

Figure 7.3: Planning for instruction and assignments.

Visit ***go.SolutionTree.com/schoolimprovement*** *for a free reproducible version of this figure.*

Planning such as this not only allows teams to take ownership of the curriculum, but it also gives teachers the ability to use their expertise and knowledge to create the cycle of learning. Teams plan to ensure a guaranteed and viable curriculum for all students while incorporating a few lessons from previous grades, if needed, or review during the learning cycle. The focus is on student learning, not on the more traditional school focus of covering the curriculum. A suggestion for staff is to plan to have Flex time after every common assessment. Flex time built into the learning cycle allows teachers to review the results of common formative assessments with students, reteach, and offer more time and support and enrichment. Figure 7.4 provides a tool for planning pacing.

Pacing Across the Learning Block *Map out days or periods of time for teaching the learning target, administering common formative assessments, and planning for flex time.*				
Monday	**Tuesday**	**Wednesday**	**Thursday**	**Friday**

Figure 7.4: Pacing plan tool.

Visit ***go.SolutionTree.com/schoolimprovement*** *for a free reproducible version of this figure.*

Assessing Student Learning

To address the second critical question of a PLC—How will we know if students have learned it?—collaborative teams create common formative assessments to monitor student learning. Teams can then use the data from the monitoring to support student learning and improve their own instruction. In *Concise Answers to Frequently Asked Questions About Professional Learning Communities at Work*, Mike Mattos, Richard DuFour, Rebecca DuFour, Robert Eaker, and Tom W. Many (2016) describe *common assessment* as:

> An assessment of student learning that uses the same instrument or a common process using the same criteria to determine the quality of student learning and student work. Teachers administer common assessments to gather evidence of the proficiency of students who are in the same curriculum and who are expected to acquire the same knowledge and skills, at the same time or within a very narrow window of time, by two or more instructors. (p. 92)

Kim Bailey and Chris Jakicic (2023) state that "common formative assessments are team-designed, intentional measures used for the purpose of monitoring student attainment of essential learning targets throughout the instructional process" (p. 24). Their book *Common Formative Assessment: A Toolkit for Professional Learning Communities at Work* (Bailey & Jakicic, 2023) include an assessment-planning template, common formative assessments checklist, and sample protocol for developing an assessment to help teams do the work of collaboratively creating common assessments. Here are the steps for creating a common formative assessment with your collaborative team that is quick to administer, appropriate for the allotted time, and easy to score.

1. Locate the priority standards and learning targets your team identified in the learning block plan.
2. Write the assessment about one to three learning targets and plan the assessment before the learning block.
3. Evaluate the cognitive demand levels of each learning target, select the best strategy for assessing the target (selected response, constructed response, a combination, or performance task), and align the assessment to the rigor of the standard.
4. Create assessment items that match the level of thinking of the learning targets (align each item to the level of demand of the learning target).

5. Agree on what mastery will look like for each item, each target, and the overall assessment, with clear success criteria.
6. Ensure the common formative assessment meets the following criteria: one or two constructed-response items, two to four selected-response items, or a combination of both. This ensures the common assessment is short, and teachers can score quickly.
7. Arrange assessment items as a cohesive, neat, organized, and easy-to-read assessment. It should include clear directions and assessment items, as well as adequate space to write and solve problems. Write the learning target on the assessment.
8. Administer the common formative assessments at the same time as other team members.
9. Collaboratively score and review the student work together as a team. (Ryan, 2023, p. 73)

Teachers can take common assessment creation to the highest level with the resource *Ethical Test Preparation* by Robert Marzano (Marzano, Dodson, Simms, & Wipf, 2021).

Using Results for Data-Driven Teamwork

In the final steps of the cycle, teacher teams work together to answer PLC critical questions three and four—What do we do if students haven't learned it, and how do we extend the learning for students who have learned it? Common formative assessments help teams determine which students need more time, support, and extension, and they also help teacher teams measure the impact their teaching is making on student learning.

Teams can use the data team process in figure 7.5 (Ryan, 2023; page 114) at the start, middle, or end of a learning cycle, stopping instruction after every common formative assessment to reteach, review, give more time and support, and extend learning.

Conclusion

The shift from isolation to a culture of collaboration in a PLC ensures teams are focused on the right work. With this collaborative focus on the right work, schools can build healthy cultures that support students and teachers learning at high levels. The time to start the right work is now!

PLC critical question three— How will we respond when some students do not learn?	
Assessment and Analysis of Student Work: • Discuss and share work samples. • Which question was the most challenging? • Which questions separate students from approaching and mastery? • How about mastery and exceeding? • Did we spend enough time during the unit on each learning target? When will we revisit?	
Instruction: • How can we change or improve instruction to meet student needs? • What was our instructional goal (element and strategy)? • What could we have done differently? • What instructional practices worked during this unit? • What can we stop doing?	
Flex time and WINN block: • What lessons can we prepare to address specific learning targets or student needs? • How will we address our targets of need with students during this time? • What is the instructional plan for Flex? WINN? • How will we include students as part of the assessment process? • When can students redo, retake, or create student-generated assessments? • Which students need more time and support?	

PLC critical question four— How will we extend the learning for students who are already proficient?	
Instruction: • How will we enrich and extend the learning for students during class using the exceeding criteria? • What is working for the students achieving at high levels?	
Flex time and WINN: • How will we continue to challenge students during flex time and college prep? • How can our team work together to take collective responsibility for all students? • Which students need extension work?	

Figure 7.5: Planning tool for giving more time and support and extension of learning.

Visit ***go.SolutionTree.com/schoolimprovement*** *for a free reproducible version of this figure.*

References and Resources

Ainsworth, L. (2003). Power standards: Identifying the standards that matter the most. Advanced Learning Press.

Bailey, K., & Jacicik, C. (2023). *Common formative assessment: A toolkit for Professional Learning Communities at Work (2nd ed.).* Bloomington, IN: Solution Tree Press.

Buffum, A., Mattos, M., & Malone, J. (2018). *Taking action: A handbook for RTI at Work.* Bloomington, IN: Solution Tree Press.

Bottiani, J. H., Duran, C. A. K., Pas, E. T., & Bradshaw, C. P. (2019). Teacher stress and burnout in urban middle schools: Associations with job demands, resources, and effective classroom practices. *Journal of School Psychology*, *77*, 36–51.

Carroll, T. (2009). The next generation of learning teams. *Phi Delta Kappan*, *91*(2), 8–13.

Chenoweth, K. (2009). It can be done, it's being done, and here's how. *Phi Delta Kappan*, *91*(1), 38–43.

Cottingham, B. W., Hough, H. J., & Myung, J. (2023). *What does it take to accelerate the learning of every child? Early insights from a CCEE school-improvement pilot.* Stanford, CA: Policy Analysis for California Education. Accessed at https://edpolicyinca.org/sites/default/files/2023-12/r_cottingham-dec2023.pdf on April 1, 2024.

Depka, E. (2017). *Raising the rigor: Effective questioning strategies and techniques for the classroom.* Bloomington, IN: Solution Tree Press.

Donohoo, J. (2017). *Collective efficacy: How educators' beliefs impact student learning.* Thousand Oaks, CA: Corwin Press.

DuFour, R., DuFour, R., Eaker, R., Many, T., & Mattos, M. (2016). *Concise answers to frequently asked questions about Professional Learning Communities at Work.* Bloomington IN: Solution Tree Press.

DuFour, R., DuFour, R., Eaker, R., Many, T., & Mattos, M. (2024). *Learning by doing: A handbook for Professional Learning Communities at Work* (3rd ed.). Bloomington, IN: Solution Tree Press.

Gruenert, S., & Whitaker, T. (2015). *School culture rewired: How to define, assess, and transform it.* Alexandria, VA: ASCD.

Hanson, H., Torres, K., Yoon, S. Y., Merrill, R., Fantz, T., & Velie, Z. (2021). *Growing together: Professional Learning Communities at Work generates achievement gains in Arkansas.* Portland, OR: Education Northwest. Accessed at https://educationnorthwest.org/sites/default/files/plc-at-work-impact-evaluation.pdf on April 1, 2024.

Hattie, J. (2015, June). *What works best in education: The politics of collaborative expertise.* London: Pearson. Accessed at www.pearson.com/content/dam/corporate/global/pearson-dot-com/files/hattie/150526_ExpertiseWEB_V1.pdf on June 20, 2022.

Hess, K. (2013). *A guide for using Webb's Depth of Knowledge with Common Core State Standards.* Albany, NY: Common Core Institute.

Kramer, S., & Schuhl, S. (2017). *School improvement for all: A how-to-guide for doing the right work.* Bloomington, IN: Solution Tree Press.

Kramer, S., & Schuhl, S. (2023). *Acceleration for all: A how-to guide for overcoming learning gaps.* Bloomington, IN: Solution Tree Press.

Love, J. (2021). *Teacher retention in high-poverty, urban schools* (Master's thesis, Concordia University, St. Paul, MN). Accessed at https://digitalcommons.csp.edu/teacher-education_masters/42 on July 5, 2022.

Many, T. W., & Sparks-Many, S. K. (2015). *Leverage: Using PLCs to promote lasting improvement in schools.* Thousand Oaks, CA: Corwin Press.

Marzano, R. (2020) *The new art and science of teaching.* Bloomington, IN: Marzano Resources.

Marzano, R., Dodson, C., Simms, J., & Wipf, J. (2022). *Ethical test preparation in the classroom.* Bloomington, IN: Marzano Resources.

Marzano, R. J., Marzano, J. S., & Pickering, D. J. (2003). *Classroom management that works. Research-based strategies for every teacher.* New York: Pearson.

Marzano, R., Warrick, P., Rains, C., & DuFour, R. (2018). *Leading a high reliability school.* Bloomington, IN: Solution Tree Press.

Montell, G. (2023). *Understanding equality and equity.* Accessed at https://edtrust.org/blog/equity-and-equality-are-not-equal on November 6, 2024.

Muhammad, A (2015). *Overcoming the achievement gap trap: Liberating mindsets to effect change.* Bloomington, IN: Solution Tree Press.

Muhammad, A. (2018). *Transforming school culture: How to overcome staff division.* (2nd ed.). Bloomington, IN: Solution Tree Press.

Muhammad, A. (2024). *The way forward: PLC at Work and the bright future of education.* Bloomington, IN: Solution Tree Press.

NYU Steinhardt School of Culture, Education, and Human Development. (2018, January 2). *New teachers, urban schools, and dropouts: A national problem.* Accessed at https://teachereducation.steinhardt.nyu.edu/new-teachers-urban-schools-dropouts on April 7, 2022.

Read On Arizona. (2024). *Case studies: Agua Caliente Elementary and Tanque Verde Elementary.* Accessed at https://readonarizona.org/case-studies/TVUSD on April 1, 2024.

Reeves, D. (2020). *Achieving equity and excellence: Immediate results from the lessons of high-poverty, high-success schools.* Bloomington, IN: Solution Tree Press.

Ryan, B. (2023). *Brilliance in the building: Effecting change in schools using the PLC process.* Bloomington, IN: Solution Tree.

Solution Tree. (2024a). *Evidence of excellence: Greater Hartford Academy of the Arts Middle School.* Accessed at www.solutiontree.com/plc-at-work/evidence-of-excellence/greater-hartford-academy on April 1, 2024.

Solution Tree. (2024b). *Evidence of excellence: Minnieville Elementary School.* Accessed at www.solutiontree.com/plc-at-work/evidence-of-excellence/minnieville on April 1, 2024.

Solution Tree. (2024c). *Evidence of excellence: Model PLC at Work and Blue Ribbon Schools.* Accessed at www.solutiontree.com/plc-at-work/evidence-of-excellence/model-plc-and-blue-ribbon-schools on April 1, 2024.

Sweeney, D., & Harris, L. (2020). *The essential guide for student-centered coaching: What every K–12 coach and school leader needs to know.* Thousand Oaks, CA: Corwin.

Mario I. Acosta, EdD, spent twenty years of his educational career as a teacher, instructional coach, assistant principal, academic director, and principal leading schools with diverse profiles in Texas. He was named the Texas 2022 Principal of the Year while principal at Westwood High School in Austin, a *U.S. News & World Report* top fifty campus and member of the High Reliability Schools Network. Dr. Acosta has had success in leading schools of all sizes, with students and teachers from a variety of backgrounds, communities, and socioeconomic statuses. He has led school turnaround in high-poverty schools in Texas at both the middle and high school levels, which yielded immediate and significant growth in student achievement data. Furthermore, under his leadership, Westwood High School was recognized as a top 1 percent campus in the United States for its academic achievement and college and career readiness.

In 2022, Dr. Acosta joined the Solution Tree–Marzano Resources team and works as an author and national presenter. He specializes in campus-level implementation of effective campus culture, High Reliability Schools, PLCs, instructional improvement, response to intervention, effective teaching strategies for English learners, and standards-referenced reporting. As a high reliability school certifier, Dr. Acosta works with K–12 schools and districts across the United States as they progress through the various certification levels. He also serves as a professor at the University of Texas at Austin, where he prepares students in the educational leadership master's degree program to become school leaders.

Dr. Acosta holds a doctorate in educational administration from the University of Texas at Austin and a superintendent certification in the state of Texas. He earned a bachelor's degree in mathematics from the University of Texas at Austin and a master's degree from Lamar University in Beaumont, Texas.

To learn more about Dr. Acosta's work, follow @marioacosta31 on X.

To book Mario I. Acosta for professional development, contact pd@SolutionTree.com

CHAPTER 8

Fostering Classroom Cultures to Motivate Learners and Give Hope to Teachers

By Mario I. Acosta

In the ever-evolving education landscape, educators stand at a pivotal juncture. We are acutely focused on students' academic success, and we intentionally work to ensure their physical and emotional well-being is a priority. We understand the importance of viewing each student as a whole child, whose academic, social, and emotional needs are intricately intertwined. The task at hand is not a simple recalibration of the old systems but a reimagining of educational practices that place the holistic development of students at its core.

This chapter explores a blueprint for catalyzing change in the classroom. It seeks to arm educators with the insights gleaned from the research on the components of an effective classroom culture to equip educators with actionable steps to foster and sustain an environment conducive to learning, growth, and positive well-being. By weaving together the threads of student motivation, behavioral research, and best practices in curriculum implementation and instructional strategies, we will construct a fabric of reform that is both resilient and responsive. When classrooms cultivate positive relationships and a sense of belonging, it reflects on the broader school environment, promoting a cohesive and thriving educational community.

The strategies in this chapter are not intended solely for students' benefit. A robust classroom culture has the potential to positively impact teacher job satisfaction, reduce teacher burnout, and enhance overall effectiveness. By rekindling the flame of enthusiasm for learning among students, we simultaneously reenergize the educators who are the custodians of their academic journey.

Approaching Student Development Holistically

Student development is multifaceted; a holistic approach is not merely advantageous but necessary. Holistic development goes beyond the conventional focus on academic achievement, advocating for the nurturing of each student's cognitive, social, emotional, and physical growth. Holistic development acknowledges that students thrive when their learning experiences go past intellectual enrichment to involve the integration of social-emotional learning (SEL) into the fabric of education, thereby cultivating competencies such as self-awareness, self-management, social awareness, relationship skills, and responsible decision making. Nurturing these competencies is crucial—they are foundational to academic success and the life skills necessary for navigating the complexities of the modern world.

A wealth of research underscores the significance of this approach. A meta-analysis by professor Joseph A. Durlak and colleagues (2011) finds that students participating in SEL programs show improved social and emotional skills, behaviors, and attitudes toward themselves and others and an eleven percentile-point gain in academic achievement. Further bolstering the case for holistic development, psychologist Mark T. Greenberg and colleagues (2003) posit that SEL is linked to significant positive impacts on children's academic performance and health-related outcomes. Education consultant and author Zaretta Hammond (2015) asserts that schools implementing SEL often report improvements in school climate, as well as increases in student and adult satisfaction. Students are better equipped to meet the challenges of their multifaceted lives when educators engage the whole child. Additionally, the Collaborative for Academic, Social, and Emotional Learning (CASEL) has extensively documented the long-term benefits of SEL, including higher rates of employment and educational fulfillment. These outcomes speak to the importance of addressing both academic and social-emotional needs in the classroom, as they are interrelated and mutually reinforcing.

Moreover, the integration of holistic education practices aligns with the understanding that intellectual growth cannot be divorced from the emotional and social context of a student's life. The American Psychological Association emphasizes the role of supportive relationships and positive learning environments in fostering resilience, a trait that enables students to adapt to adversity and thrive.

The holistic approach to student development is grounded in a wealth of research indicating that when schools invest in the full spectrum of student growth—academic, social, and emotional—the dividends are comprehensive and enduring. Students become more proficient learners and more capable, compassionate, and well-rounded individuals. This approach is not merely an educational strategy; it is a profound investment in the future of our society.

Developing an Effective Classroom Culture

For schools to develop students holistically, teachers need to create classroom cultures that are conducive to this approach. Too often, the pressures placed on the school system cause educators to default to the long-standing practices of industrious school environments. According to authors Mike Ruyle, Libby Child, and Nancy Dome (2022):

> Students in industrialized educational systems are part of a typically passive learning environment. They often take little ownership of their learning in that they are grouped based on their chronological age, respond to teacher direction, and submit required assignments to earn enough credits to move through school and, eventually, graduate. (p. 64)

This industrialization of educational environments impacts student engagement and ownership.

Effective classroom cultures are rooted in authentic student engagement in which they take an active role in both their learning and personal development. While many factors contribute to student achievement, the quality of the classroom teacher is the most influential factor in determining the success of individual students. In fact, educational researcher and author Robert J. Marzano (2017) asserts that effective teachers enhance student performance, whereas ineffective teachers fail to produce the same positive outcomes. The impact of teaching quality on student achievement is substantial and unmistakable. To that end, teachers can create classroom environments that maximize their students' success and, in turn, increase their own efficacy and job satisfaction.

Effective school cultures consist of teachers who are deeply committed to the school's mission and values, consistently demonstrating high expectations and unwavering dedication to student success (Muhammad, 2018). These teachers and teams of teachers, who educational author and speaker Anthony Muhammad (2018) calls Believers, are called on to ensure the overall school culture values effective individual classroom cultures. It is important, however, to accentuate the fact that, due to the inherent power dynamic in the teacher-student relationship, "we can confidently say that the classroom culture is determined by the teacher" (Gruenert & Whitaker, 2017, p. 69). Teachers have a direct influence over their students, impacting each student's mindset and outcomes both academically and personally. Teachers are encouraged to audit their current classrooms to ensure the existing culture supports learning and growth for each of their students.

The six components of an effective classroom culture include: (1) creating a safe classroom environment, (2) setting and holding high expectations that motivate learners, (3) using brain-based instructional strategies to individualize the learning process, (4) managing behavior effectively, (5) building relationships with students, and (6) engaging parents. By adhering to these components, educators can create a classroom culture that promotes growth, learning, and positive behavior, fostering a supportive community for all students and their families.

Creating a Safe Classroom Environment

A safe classroom environment is fundamental for student success as it nurtures a sense of security and belonging that is crucial for academic engagement and learning. The safety of the classroom environment is pivotal in ensuring the emotional and physical safety of all students, which is non-negotiable (Marzano, Scott, Boogren, & Newcomb, 2017). When students feel secure, they can direct their focus toward learning, and educators can dedicate their efforts to teaching and fostering an optimal educational experience. The role of emotion in learning is pivotal. Emotions can gatekeep the information that reaches our long-term memory. These methods boost academic performance and contribute to a positive classroom culture where students feel engaged and invested in their learning journey.

In the quest to enhance classroom culture, educators are increasingly turning to SEL strategies as pivotal elements of instructional design. SEL provides a framework for understanding and managing emotions, setting and achieving positive goals, feeling and showing empathy for others, establishing and maintaining positive relationships, and making responsible decisions. This supports learners' psychological safety to access the curriculum. It follows that high-level learning for all will only occur with a paradigm shift that allows educators to "focus their energies on the brain, body, and the overall wellness of the students in their schools" (Ruyle, Child, & Dome, 2022, p. 29). By integrating SEL into daily practices, educators create a supportive environment that nurtures students' abilities to navigate the social complexities of the classroom and beyond. This can be as simple as starting the day with a check-in, allowing students to express their feelings and prepare for learning, or as structured as incorporating SEL curricula that teach and practice these skills in a dedicated manner.

To weave these strategies into daily classroom practices, teachers can begin by creating routines that incorporate SEL principles. For instance, starting each lesson with a brief mindfulness exercise can calm the nervous system and prime the brain for learning. Group work can be structured to foster collaboration and empathy, while reflective activities can help students internalize and articulate their learning experiences.

Implementing Practices That Motivate Learners

Educators can employ practical methods that start with setting clear expectations to foster an effective classroom culture. These expectations should be cocreated with students to give them a sense of ownership and responsibility. When students are involved in the creation of classroom rules and norms, they are more likely to adhere to them and encourage their peers to do the same.

Teachers are encouraged to determine the right level of challenge, ensure proficiency in foundational skills, offer positive affirmations, and believe their students can learn. Setting and holding high expectations for each student communicates a belief in their potential and sets a standard for them to aspire to. The expectation level that a teacher holds for an individual student influences their interactions with that student. As Marzano (2017) explains, "The greater the teacher's expectations for students, the more teachers challenge and interact with them" (p. 97). When teachers are acutely aware of their expectation level for every student, a classroom environment manifests where excellence is the norm, and students are motivated to reach their full potential.

Creating a learning-conducive environment is intrinsically linked to fostering student motivation and encouraging positive behavior. A classroom culture that promotes motivation and engagement is not built overnight—it is cultivated through consistent, intentional practices that recognize and respond to students' diverse needs.

The connection between classroom culture and student motivation is well-established in educational research. For example, a 2021 study by researcher

Xiaowei Tu (2021) emphasizes that a positive classroom culture that prioritizes psychological safety significantly boosts student engagement and participation, which are critical components of motivation. Similarly, another study by professor and author Joseph Zajda (2023) discusses how various motivation theories impact student engagement and performance, demonstrating that a supportive and engaging classroom environment is crucial for motivating students and enhancing their academic success. Furthermore, research by Chen and Hwang (2022) has found that structured classroom learning environments positively influence student motivation through improved self-regulation and engagement. These findings underscore the importance of fostering a positive classroom culture to enhance student motivation and overall academic outcomes.

A positive classroom culture affects a student's desire to learn and participate, making motivation intrinsic rather than extrinsic. Researcher Mayuri Borah (2021) details the impact of student motivation on learning outcomes:

> The role of teachers in motivating learners cannot be overemphasized. It is recommended that teachers should create an active learning environment that enhances students' perceived autonomy and competence, providing students with choices and opportunities for self-directed learning, and planning learning activities that might increase their feeling of mastery. (p. 552)

Student engagement levels rise when they feel like part of a learning community where their ideas are valued and their presence matters. This sense of belonging can significantly reduce negative behaviors and enhance student motivation.

Another method is to personalize learning experiences. Students are naturally more motivated when they see the relevance of their learning to their own lives. This can be done by integrating students' interests and backgrounds into the curriculum and by providing choices in how they learn and demonstrate their understanding. Educators and authors Steve Gruenert and Todd Whitaker (2017) offer teachers the following questions to support interesting and relevant instructional design, "Does the subject matter make sense? Is it interesting and relevant to students' interests and priorities, inside and outside of the class?" (p. 60). Personalization acknowledges students as individuals and respects their unique learning paths.

In addition to personalizing learning, educators can use goal-setting and self-assessment techniques to foster self-motivation. By setting achievable, incremental goals, students can experience a sense of accomplishment that fuels their desire to continue learning. Self-assessment allows students to reflect on their learning processes, recognize their progress, and identify areas for improvement.

Positive reinforcement is also key in encouraging desirable behavior. Recognizing and celebrating successes, however small, can have a profound impact on student self-esteem and motivation. This reinforcement should be specific, immediate, and consistent, ensuring that students understand what behaviors are being recognized.

Additionally, providing opportunities for students to collaborate and learn from each other can enhance motivation. Collaborative learning builds a supportive community and allows students to take on leadership roles, challenge each other, and share in the joy of collective achievement (Loes, 2022).

The classroom culture is the bedrock on which student motivation and behavior are built. Educators can nurture an environment that motivates students to learn and behave positively by setting high expectations, personalizing learning, implementing goal-setting and self-assessment, providing positive reinforcement, and encouraging collaboration. The result is a self-sustaining cycle where motivated behavior begets a positive culture, which in turn further enhances motivation.

Using Brain-Based Instructional Practices to Individualize Learning

Brain-based learning strategies stem from the understanding that certain pedagogical techniques align with the brain's natural learning processes, thereby improving retention and understanding. For instance, incorporating movement into lessons can boost neural activity and engagement (Wilson & Conyers, 2014). This might involve students acting out a historical event or using gestures to represent mathematical concepts, thereby solidifying their learning through action. Additionally, *spaced repetition*, which distributes learning over time, and *interleaving*, which mixes different but related topics, are methods that can greatly enhance memory and recall, as they require the brain to actively reconstruct knowledge.

To individualize the learning process, educators can employ differentiated instruction, formative assessments, and scaffolded learning tasks that are responsive to students' varying abilities, interests, and learning profiles. Differentiated instruction allows teachers to tailor their teaching strategies to meet students' diverse needs, while formative assessments provide ongoing feedback that can be used to tailor instruction to the specific skill needs serving each student's learning progress. Provide students with individual learning opportunities to support their learning progression.

Curriculum and instruction best practices are continually evolving in K–12 education. Marzano's (2017) *The New Art and Science of Teaching* offers a contemporary framework that aligns with a standards-based classroom approach, emphasizing clarity, feedback, and pedagogical flexibility while ensuring a holistic brain-based approach to curricular and instructional design.

To implement Marzano's strategies, educators can focus on designing and delivering lessons that align with educational standards while remaining responsive to students' diverse needs. This fosters robust, well-rounded students by preparing them for both academic success and success beyond the K–12 classroom environment. Figure 8.1 details instructional action steps based on this framework.

DESIGNING RIGOROUS, STANDARDS-BASED LESSONS

Familiarize yourself with the specific standards and learning goals for your grade level and subject area.

Use backward design to plan lessons, starting with the end goal in mind and planning assessments before instructional strategies.

Create scales and rubrics that align with the standards to make the learning objectives transparent to students.

CONDUCTING DIRECT INSTRUCTION LESSONS

Use a mix of teacher-led instruction and student-centered activities to cater to different learning styles.

Incorporate multimedia and technology to enhance understanding and engagement.

CONDUCTING PRACTICING AND DEEPENING LESSONS

Utilize a variety of structured practice activities that challenge students at different levels, ensuring they apply concepts in multiple contexts to enhance skill mastery.

Encourage students to systematically examine similarities and differences among concepts, which can lead to a deeper understanding and an increased ability to apply knowledge in various situations.

Implement error analysis in practice activities to help students learn from mistakes, fostering a growth mindset and enhancing their problem-solving skills.

IMPLEMENTING ENGAGING INSTRUCTIONAL STRATEGIES	Employ interactive learning strategies, such as cooperative learning, problem-based learning, and discussions, to promote student engagement. Differentiate instruction to meet the needs of all learners, providing both support and challenge as needed.
USING EFFECTIVE QUESTIONING AND FEEDBACK	Develop questioning strategies that encourage high levels of participation and higher-order thinking. Provide immediate and specific feedback to support student learning and growth. Utilize ongoing formative assessments to understand each student's skill strengths and areas for growth.
ENHANCING STUDENT METACOGNITION	Teach students to consider about their own thinking and learning processes. Use reflective exercises to help students become more aware of their cognitive strategies and how to improve them.

Source: Adapted from Marzano, 2017.

Figure 8.1: Strategies for effective brain-based instructional planning.

This approach to curriculum and instruction design not only aids in content mastery but also in the development of critical thinking, problem-solving, and self-regulatory skills that are essential for students' success both inside and outside the classroom. By addressing students' holistic needs through thoughtful planning, educators foster environments that support emotional and social growth alongside academic achievements. This integrative strategy enriches classroom culture by promoting a sense of community, encouraging student engagement, and nurturing well-rounded individuals who are prepared to navigate the world's complexities.

Managing Behavior Effectively

Effective behavior management is also crucial in cultivating a productive learning environment. A well-considered discipline plan is central to an effective classroom culture, serving as a foundation for a proactive and effectively managed classroom. According to Marzano (2003), "classroom management is one of the critical ingredients to effective teaching" (p. 6). Develop a behavior management plan that includes positive reinforcement and clear consequences. Implement this plan consistently and review it periodically with students. This can involve establishing clear rules and routines that are consistently applied, along with positive reinforcement to encourage students to make appropriate behavioral choices. It's essential to employ fair and equitable practices that teach students self-regulation and conflict-resolution skills. The modern educator's classroom is a dynamic environment where diverse needs and backgrounds converge. Effective classroom management in this context is less about maintaining order and more about cultivating a culture of respect and inclusivity. Such an environment naturally minimizes truancy and disruptions as students feel valued and motivated to engage.

To achieve this, educators must employ advanced classroom management strategies that are responsive to the evolving educational landscape. One such strategy involves the implementation of positive behavioral interventions and supports, which focuses on proactive strategies to promote positive behavior. Educators can foster a sense of community and shared responsibility by recognizing and rewarding positive behaviors rather than merely punishing negative ones.

Another advanced approach is the incorporation of restorative practices. These practices emphasize the importance of relationships and community in the educational process. When disruptions occur, restorative practices seek to understand and address the root causes of the behavior, rather than simply dispensing punitive measures. This approach encourages accountability and empathy, as students learn to understand the impact of their actions on others and are involved in the process of making amends.

Creating a respectful and inclusive classroom also involves designing lessons that are relevant to students' lives. This can be achieved by integrating culturally responsive teaching, which recognizes the importance of referencing students' cultures in all aspects of learning. By doing so, students feel a sense of belonging and are less likely to disengage or act out.

Additionally, modern educators can leverage technology to enhance classroom management. Digital platforms can be used to track behavior in real-time, allowing for immediate feedback and adjustments. These systems can also facilitate communication between teachers, students, and parents, creating a more interconnected and supportive educational community.

A classroom that is managed effectively also relies on clear and consistent routines. These routines provide a predictable structure that can reduce anxiety and mitigate behavioral issues. Students are more likely to exhibit self-regulation and engagement when they understand what is expected of them and what they can expect from their environment. A study conducted by researchers Keith C. Herman, Wendy M. Reinke, Nianbo Dong, and Catherine P. Bradshaw (2022) finds, "Effective classroom management can improve student achievement, in part, by increasing the amount of time students are attentive, on-task, and exposed to instruction" (p. 156).

Advanced classroom management strategies for the modern educator are multifaceted and require a shift from a reactive to a proactive stance. By embracing positive behavioral interventions and supports, restorative practices, culturally responsive teaching, and the judicious use of technology, educators can create learning spaces that are respectful, inclusive, and conducive to the success of all students. These strategies mitigate truancy and disruptions and contribute to a positive and productive classroom atmosphere where every student can thrive.

Building Relationships With Students

Additionally, the teacher's ability to build positive relationships is a critical factor for a thriving classroom culture. As educator and school psychologist Allen N. Mendler (2021) explains, teachers can foster these relationships by showing genuine interest in their students' lives, valuing their input, and providing support and encouragement while letting students know they are more important than their behavior by inviting feedback and offering support to students in times of crisis or uncertainty. Dedicate time to know your students personally. Building these trusting relationships can be accomplished by getting to know them through greeting them daily, one-on-one meetings, interest surveys, or simply engaging in daily conversations. Establishing relationships with students can take on many forms.

Studies validate the significance of forming personal connections with students to enhance their sense of worth and overall engagement in the classroom. Positive student-teacher relationships foster a sense of belonging, which directly correlates with increased school engagement and academic performance (Allen et al., 2021). Furthermore, students are more motivated to learn when they feel valued and understood by their teachers, demonstrating that personalized attention boosts both emotional and academic outcomes (Urdan & Schoenfelder, 2006).

The relationships a teacher develops with their students become an essential component of the classroom culture. Students are a central component, and their willingness to buy into the established beliefs and expected behaviors determines the health of the classroom's culture. This phenomenon manifests when a single teacher uses the same instructional and management strategies with different groups of students yielding varied results. Educators can attest to the fact that no two classes are identical and do not respond to strategies in the same manner. Teachers must therefore rely on creating strong positive relationships with all students to encourage them to actively engage in the desired classroom culture.

Engaging Parents

Engaging families and the school community is vital in creating an effective classroom culture. Educators can actively increase family engagement and foster collaborative approaches with community members. Teachers need to create multiple channels for parent-teacher communication. A first step in this process is to regularly update parents on their child's progress and involve them in the learning process. Creating conditions for positive relationships extends beyond the classroom to include parents and caregivers. Communication is key; regular, open dialogue about a student's progress and ways to support learning at home can reinforce the partnership between educators and families.

For a healthy classroom culture to exist, educators must redefine the paradigm for parent-school relations. Traditional methods of parental involvement place parents in the role of helping teachers and educators to "fix" students according to the school's agenda regarding their child's education. To create an effective classroom culture, teachers would be well-served to shift the parental role; educational leadership researcher Ann M. Ishimaru (2020) describes as a new kind of relationship that designates parents and families as change agents who possess specialized expertise in their cultural and linguistic repertoires, lived experiences, social and cultural resources, and community leadership. Researchers Muhammad Khalifa, Noelle W. Arnold, and Whitney Newcomb (2015) suggest:

> When there is positive rapport between school and parents, parents and educators have a better understanding and trust of each other. This accomplishes three key things: Reduces parents' resistance to educators or reforms; Mobilizes parent support for these reforms; and Increases educators' knowledge of the parents they are beginning to serve. (p. 24)

By implementing these strategies, teachers can work alongside parents and community members to support students' learning and well-being, strengthening the overall classroom culture.

By fostering positive relationships and redefining parent-school dynamics, teachers and parents can become Believers dedicated and invested in the shared mission of student success. When parents and educators collaborate as partners—leveraging their unique insights and cultural backgrounds—they build mutual trust and understanding. This partnership transforms parents into active change agents, enriching the school community with diverse perspectives and resources. Consequently, this collaborative effort not only enhances student learning and well-being but also fortifies a vibrant and effective classroom culture. Through this unified approach, both teachers and parents commit to the collective goal of nurturing and empowering every student, embodying the true essence of a supportive and engaged educational environment.

Analyzing Teacher Efficacy and Job Satisfaction

Teachers' self-efficacy can be significantly bolstered by the very act of cultivating an effective classroom culture. By setting high expectations for each student, educators inherently affirm their belief in every student's potential, which reflects in their perception of their own effectiveness.

Employing evidence-based teaching practices tailored to students' individual learning needs enhances student outcomes and reinforces teachers' confidence in their instructional methods. The teacher's belief in their capabilities is further solidified as students respond positively to these personalized strategies.

Teachers can also develop self-efficacy through effective behavior management processes. When teachers create environments conducive to learning and successfully manage their classrooms, the smooth operation of the class is a testament to their competence and skills. A study conducted by researchers Robert M. Klassen and Ming Ming Chiu (2010) posits, "Teachers with high levels of self-efficacy for classroom management and instructional strategies reported higher levels of job satisfaction" (p. 749). Teachers who have developed the skills and place a strong focus on well-managed and engaged students show significantly higher levels of job satisfaction than teachers who experience ongoing stress from low engagement and negative student behavior manifesting from weaker classroom management application.

Focusing on building positive relationships within the classroom, teachers establish trust and respect. These relationships often lead to better classroom dynamics and improved student behavior, thereby contributing to a teacher's sense of accomplishment and professional satisfaction. According to researchers Rebecca J. Collie, Jennifer D. Shapka, and Nancy E. Perry (2012), one of the most powerful school-based predictor variables in determining teacher efficacy was a teachers' comfort in implementing SEL. It was negatively associated with stress related to students' behavior and discipline and positively associated with teaching efficacy and job satisfaction. These teachers may then experience more positive forms of healthy teacher-student relationships, effective classroom management, a healthy classroom environment, and effective SEL implementation, which may help them to experience lower stress, greater teaching efficacy, and greater job satisfaction.

Additionally, creating conditions for positive relationships between educators, students, and parents extends the impact of a teacher's efficacy beyond the classroom walls. Engaging with parents strengthens the educational triangle, leading to a more supportive learning environment for students and a greater sense of community and achievement for teachers.

In essence, the creation of an effective classroom culture is not a one-way street; it is a dynamic process that enhances student learning and, concurrently, boosts teacher efficacy and job satisfaction. Teachers' belief in their impact grows when they see the fruits of their labor in their students' success and the support of the school community, completing a positive feedback loop that elevates the educational experience for everyone involved.

Conclusion

This chapter provides a framework for fostering a classroom culture that is both conducive to learning and focuses on the whole student. Educators lay the groundwork for student achievement within a healthy classroom culture by creating a safe, structured setting; holding high expectations; emphasizing student motivation; using brain-based teaching methods; and fostering strong relationships. They engage with students' families and the community while integrating social-emotional learning to support students' holistic development. As educators, our mission extends to nurturing every aspect of our students' development, ensuring their success inside and outside of the classroom. As you embark on this journey, you are not just teaching; you are empowering a generation to learn, grow, and succeed.

References and Resources

Allen, K.-A., Slaten, C. D., Arslan, G., Roffey, S., Craig, H., & Vella-Brodrick, D. A. (2021). School belonging: The importance of student and teacher relationships. In M. L. Kern & M. L. Wehmeyer (Eds.), *The Palgrave handbook of positive education* (pp. 525–550). Palgrave Macmillan/Springer Nature.

Borah, M. (2021). Motivation in learning. *Journal of Critical Reviews, 8*(2), 550–552.

Canter, L., & Canter, M. (2001). *Assertive discipline: Positive behavior management for today's classroom.* Los Angeles, CA: Canter & Associates.

Chen, Y. J., & Hwang, F. M. (2022). Self-regulation matters: Examining the relationship between classroom learning environments and student motivation through structural equation modeling. *Social Psychology of Education.* https://doi.org/10.1007/s11218-021-09666-3

Collie, R. J., Shapka, J. D., & Perry, N. E. (2012). School climate and social-emotional learning: Predicting teacher stress, job satisfaction, and teaching efficacy. *Journal of Educational Psychology, 104*(4), 1189–1204.

Durlak, J. A., Weissberg, R. P., Dymnicki, A. B., Taylor, R. D., & Schellinger, K. B. (2011). The impact of enhancing students' social and emotional learning: A meta-analysis of school-based universal interventions. *Child Development, 82*(1), 405–432.

Greenberg, M. T., Weissberg, R. P., O'Brien, M. U., Zins, J. E., Fredricks, L., Resnik, H., et al. (2003). Enhancing school-based prevention and youth development through coordinated social, emotional, and academic learning. *American Psychologist, 58*(6–7), 466–474.

Gruenert, S., & Whitaker, T. (2017). *School culture recharged: Strategies to energize your staff and culture.* Arlington, VA: ASCD.

Hammond, Z. (2015). *Culturally responsive teaching and the brain: Promoting authentic engagement and rigor among culturally and linguistically diverse students.* Thousand Oaks, CA: Corwin Press.

Herman, K. C., Reinke, W. M., Dong, N., & Bradshaw, C. P. (2022). Can effective classroom behavior management increase student achievement in middle school? Findings from a group randomized trial. *Journal of Educational Psychology, 114*(1), 144–160.

Ishimaru, A. M. (2020). *Just schools: Building equitable collaborations with families and communities.* New York: Teachers College Press.

Khalifa, M., Arnold, N. W., & Newcomb, W. (2015). Understand and advocate for communities first. *Kappan, 96*(7), 20–25.

Klassen, R. M., & Chiu, M. M. (2010). Effects on teachers' self-efficacy and job satisfaction: Teacher gender, years of experience, and job stress. *American Psychological Association, 102*(3), 741–756.

Loes, C. N. (2022). The effect of collaborative learning on academic motivation. *Teaching and Learning Inquiry, 10.* https://doi.org/10.20343/teachlearninqu.10.4

Marzano, R. J. (2003). *Classroom management that works: Research-based strategies for every teacher*. Arlington, VA: ASCD.

Marzano, R. J. (2017). *The new art and science of teaching*. Bloomington, IN: Solution Tree Press.

Marzano, R. J., Scott, D., Boogren, T. H., & Newcomb, M. L. (2017). *Motivating and inspiring students: Strategies to awaken the learner*. Bloomington, IN: Marzano Resources.

Mendler, A. N. (2021). *Motivating students who don't care: Proven strategies to engage all learners* (2nd ed.). Bloomington, IN: Solution Tree Press.

Muhammad, A. (2018). *Transforming school culture: How to overcome staff division* (2nd ed.). Bloomington, IN: Solution Tree Press.

Ruyle, M., Child, L., & Dome, N. (2022). *The school wellness wheel: A framework addressing trauma, culture, and mastery to raise student achivement*. Bloomington, IN: Marzano Resources.

Tu, X. (2021). The role of classroom culture and psychological safety in EFL students' engagement. *Frontiers in Psychology*, *12*, Article 760903. https://doi.org/10.3389/fpsyg.2021.760903

Urdan, T., & Schoenfelder, E. (2006). Classroom effects on student motivation: Goal structures, social relationships, and competence beliefs. *Journal of School Psychology*, *44*(5), 331–349. https://doi.org/10.1016/j.jsp.2006.04.003

Wilson, D., & Conyers, M. (2014). *Move your body, grow your brain* [Blog post]. Accessed at www.edutopia.org/blog/move-body-grow-brain-donna-wilson on August 23, 2024.

Zajda, J. (2023). *Globalisation and dominant models of motivation theories in education*. New York: Springer.

Index

V

W

Z

Culture Keepers
Anthony Muhammad, Editor
Top educators and contributors provide guidance on how to transform school culture post-pandemic, how to confront staff resistance and chronic absenteeism, and how to address achievement gaps in English learners schoolwide, among other pertinent topics.
BKG215

Transforming School Culture, Second Edition
Anthony Muhammad
The second edition of this best-selling resource delivers powerful new insight into the four types of educators and how to work with each group to create thriving schools. The book also includes Dr. Muhammad's latest research and a new chapter of frequently asked questions.
BKF793

Time for Change
Anthony Muhammad and Luis F. Cruz
Exceptional leaders have four distinctive skills: strong communication, the ability to build trust, the ability to increase the skills of those they lead, and a results orientation. Time for Change offers powerful guidance for those seeking to develop and strengthen these skills.
BKF683

Learning By Doing, Fourth Edition
Richard DuFour, Rebecca DuFour, Robert Eaker, Thomas W. Many, Mike Mattos, and Anthony Muhammad
In this fourth edition of the bestseller *Learning by Doing*, the authors use updated research and time-tested knowledge to address current education challenges, from learning gaps exacerbated by the COVID-19 pandemic to the need to drive a highly effective multitiered system of supports.
BKG169

Visit SolutionTree.com or call 800.733.6786 to order.